*To my mother, Jeanne, always a traveler . . .*

# Contents

# 1

## *Introduction*

If you visit Key West only briefly, come unprepared, or are unlucky in a few ways, you may miss Key West entirely. You might find it hot, crowded, trashy, sinful, and expensive. And there isn't anyplace to park. On the other hand, with some preparation and good advice, enough time and an open mind, it's likely you'll become enchanted by the rippling color of sea and sky, the clattering trees and crowing roosters, and the bizarre pulse of human activity found nowhere else on earth.

Key West is not for everyone; but there is something here for almost anyone. The water, in scintillating shades of blue too many to name, invites everyone below the surface where snorkelers (even first–timers) and scuba divers can witness the coral reefs and wrecks, the turtles and rays, the myriad fish in colors beyond imagining. You can troll for the great monsters of the deep out in the Gulf Stream—marlin, tuna, sailfish; or trick the permit or tarpon in the shallow flats among the mangroves and keys with a fly or bait. This is a kayaker's and sailor's paradise. The occasional thunderstorm, a circus of bird life, and the symphony of the sunset makes this a photographer's dream. You might come for the remarkable history revealed here, the museums and forts, sites of piracy, Civil War military construction, the legacies of the Spanish and Cubans, the influence of spongers, wreckers and ghosts. You could spend a week of rainy days crawling the many art galleries found in Old Town. It's possible to eat every meal at a different place for weeks, every ethnic variety, taste things you've never tasted before: hogfish, conch, Key West pink shrimp, banana chicken with walnuts, key lime garlic oysters. In January and February it is often one hundred degrees warmer here than back in Fargo or Oshkosh or Fort Wayne—reason enough to come.

Key West is unique, neither American nor Caribbean. It is a surprisingly small (two by four mile) island at the end of US 1, a three hour drive from the mainland. It sits atop America's only living, very treacherous, reef, adjacent to busy shipping lanes and the Gulf Stream, nearly seven hundred miles south of Atlanta. Pirates, poets, painters, the dreamers and the lost have been coming here for almost two hundred years. The island has attracted residents as diverse as John James Audubon, Harry Truman, Thomas Edison, John Dewey, Jimmy Buffet, and Tennessee Williams.

My first visit to Key West, more than twenty years ago, was an opportunity to exercise my new scuba diving certificate, and to attend the annual Literary Festival. As a rather clueless and rural Midwesterner, I was hypnotized by the weightless underwater floating along the reef, among the gaudy fish and dancing corals. The sweet aroma of flowers in the balmy night, the scent of grilled catch of the day, the stories on every barstool in town were almost too much to believe. And the chance to casually chat with writers I'd read in school—well, I felt I'd found a very special place. I have since been coming in all seasons for all reasons;

in April for permit and bonefish, to watch the tarpon turn in the sunlight, the rays leap from the blue and silver water; in July for Hemingway Days and to run the 5K, cleansed by the heat and humidity. I once flew a small plane through snow and fog, all the way from northern Minnesota, arriving in time for Thanksgiving dinner on the patio at The Hard Rock Café (not my choice). I have come with any willing friend or relative, for romantic retreats; and I have come, as often as not, by myself; but I've never felt alone here.

My biases will be obvious as we go along; I am a frequent visitor, but still an outsider; my Key West will not be yours. I come from northern Minnesota where the winters are in black and white and very long, the trees leafless seven months of the year, the lakes frozen almost that long, and the only poet around is your neighbor's aunt with the feathered hat; where fine dining is meatloaf and a "nice" piece of pie. Forgive me if I gush over the warm mornings and vibrant colors, characters I'd never meet at home, an appetizer called "devils on horseback." I prefer sailing, kayaking, swimming, and biking to power boats and mopeds, the noise and machinery that separate us from one another and the natural world. I don't own an I-pod or a cell phone. I like the Cuban notion that coffee is served with a place to sit and conversation. Although some of my listings and suggestions are extensive, they are not complete or exhaustive. Many excellent inns, restaurants, sailing charters, and odd corners of this island will still be yours to discover. What follows, in brief, are a few important suggestions.

Come for a few days, three at a minimum. If you drive down from Miami, and everyone should once, know that the journey is scenic but longer than just the miles; allow four hours or more each way. People sometimes drive from south Florida to Key West as a day trip. They arrive in mid-day gridlock, can't find a place to park, jump out for a picture at the southernmost point, leave short of any discovery, and head back against the traffic, the sunset in the rear-view mirror. Don't do that.

Ditch the car. If you drive down, park it for the duration. Better yet, fly in or come by ferry or shuttle, and once here, rely on your feet or a bicycle or the taxis. Key West is flat and everything is within a short bike ride. With a cable and lock, a little night light and a basket, a bike is your ticket to freedom in Key West.

Stay in Old Town, that part of the island southwest of White Street. Travel agents and the internet may lead you to the chain motels on the north end, New Town, a distressing strip mall and parking lot kind of place, possessed with the urgency of the island's arrivals and departures. It's a long walk from there to anywhere interesting; you might as well still be in Homestead.

In Old Town, stay in an historic old inn. They capture the essence of life in Key West and are an attraction in and of themselves, woven into the fabric of Key West history which is to be found on any lane, in any city lot or old building: Here is where Henry Faulkner lived with his pet goat and gave Tennessee Williams painting lessons. Here is where Count von Cosel made love to the corpse Elena. This charming inn was once a bordello. Or, this is where the mayor set out to water-ski to Cuba, where Thomas Edison experimented with explosives, where Truman Capote offered to sign the penis of an autograph seeker's outraged husband.

Get out on the water. Looking at it is not like being

on it. Kayak, snorkel, or go on an afternoon sail or a sunset cruise on a schooner. Feel the roll, smell the living water, see the dolphins, immerse yourself in the fantastic sea—so much easier than you may think. Eat it too. The catch of the day, blackened, grilled, or pecan crusted will taste otherworldly, like nothing you've had back home.

Learn something about this place while you're here. Tour the Little White House, Fort Zachary Taylor, Hemingway's House, the Customs House and the East Martello Museum. Ride the Conch Train. It's touristy, but you are a tourist and for now that's okay.

Be tolerant, accepting, and open-minded. This is not like everywhere else and that's why many people live here. The strolling drag queen who looks vaguely like your truck-driving brother-in-law, the wizard sleeping under the bougainvillea, the man sharing a table with his dog, are all part of Key West's One Human Family. Get to know them.

Key West is wondrous and strange, gay and macho, sexy and sad. It is a place of rainbows and waterspouts, shipwrecks and hurricanes, flying fish and jumping rays, a theater of natural beauty created out of thin air, light and water, of lives acted out successfully and desperately, unfolding at the end of the road. It is a place which, in ways you might not yet understand, could change your life.

*"Flagler's Folly"* —The railroad from the mainland was completed in 1912, wiped out in the hurricane of 1935.

# 2
## *History*

Key West has always been seductively appealing, valuable, vulnerable, and dangerous due to three natural factors: It is on the backbone of an ancient coral reef, the third longest reef on the planet. It is adjacent to the great Gulf Stream, biggest river in the world, the deep blue highway of the great fish and the fast lane for ships sailing east and north to the east coast of the United States and Europe. And Key West is just barely, and tantalizingly so, accessible to the mainland of the United States, 110 miles across the stepping stones of more than forty keys.

These forty-some named and mostly inhabited keys are among the 800 other, mostly smaller keys, set along the reef which runs from Key Biscayne, past Key West and out to the Dry Tortugas, 70 miles west of Key West. The reef rises to just below the surface in places, a hazard for ships fleeing hurricanes or pirates. Then it plunges deep towards the Gulf Stream which runs parallel to the south. In the throes of a 1622 hurricane, the Spanish treasure galleon *Atocha*, loaded with gold bars, coins, 47 tons of silver, and 70 pounds of emeralds, sank, as did so many other ships before and after, in the shallows of the reef. The recent recovery of the ship's phenomenal riches is one of Key West's most remarkable stories.

In 1533 Ponce de Leon arrived, naming the Keys The Orphans, but the name that stuck for Key West, at the time, was Cayo Hueso – Bone Key. There may have been bones, perhaps the bones of slaughtered Indians, the Caloosas, or maybe just shells and coral. At any rate, by the 1700s, hueso was dropped in favor of oeso – west. The Spanish hueso sounded like "west" to the English speaking Bahamians who fished and settled the area, and Key West it has been ever since.

In 1819 John Whitehead, shipper and businessman en route from New York to Mobile, spied Key West from his anchored ship. He learned it had a deep water harbor, considered its position in the shipping lanes from southern ports to the east coast, so close to Havana, and he let the island cast its spell over him. Spain owned the island at the time of Whitehead's "discovery," but by July of 1821 ownership had been transferred to the United States in a ceremony in Pensacola, presided over by Andrew Jackson. John Whitehead and his partner John Simonton were then able to buy the island from the legal owner, John Salas, for $2000. Salas promptly rushed off to Georgia and sold it again. The double-dealing was quickly revealed and remedied. But the land speculation, entrepreneurial maneuvering, scandal and corruption continue to make news in *The Citizen*, Key West's daily paper, on a regular basis.

The strategic but hazardous area was buzzing with pirates and privateers (government authorized pirates, sent to seize ships of other countries). The goal of Whitehead, Simonton and other investors was to establish Key West as a customs port, a base for security and defense, and a center of commerce. The navy sent the West Indies Squadron after the pirates but they failed in the shallow and confusing waters and keys.

*Clockwise from upper left: The Custom House, Fort Zachary Taylor, The Lighthouse, cannon balls at Zachary Taylor.*

In 1823, David Porter, a larger–than-life character who had achieved fame in the War of 1812 and in battle against Jean Lafitte at New Orleans, was dispatched to Key West by the navy. He established a base on the island, as well as Martial Law. His first goal was to eradicate the pirates. He did so within months, using a fleet of both deep and shallow water vessels which enabled the crews to chase the pirates into the myriad shallow coves and mangroves.   He was nasty and arrogant (not to be confused with the beloved medical officer Joseph Porter, fifty years later), the first in a line of moralists who saw Key west as loathsome, untamed, and in need of correction.   Not only did he eliminate the pirates within months of his arrival; he also established the whipping post, laid roads, cut down trees, took possession of and killed the locals' farm animals. If Porter arrived today he would likely slaughter the chickens, shut down the tattoo parlors, outlaw drinking, flog the gays, and jail the strippers.

The bugs, yellow fever, and heat finally drove Mr. Porter away, but not before he arrested an aging Mr. Mallory (he and his wife had established a boardinghouse and you'll be watching the sunset at Mallory Square) for selling cider! Mallory paid a fine in lieu of 39 lashes. Porter and sidekick Lt. Frederick Varnum also tried to corner the wrecking business (salvaging reef-wrecked ships) but local wreckers would have none of that.

By 1830 the Navy had left and the city of 500 had incorporated. William Whitehead, John's younger half-brother, laid out the grid of streets which is now Old Town. Most of these street names are those of family, friends, and relatives whom we'll meet in the next chapter when we discuss the map of Key West.

This lucrative business of wrecking also involved the splitting of the booty with insurance companies, shippers, and judges. It became the main industry in the 1820s, providing not only wealth but drama and lore as well. Various opportunities for fraud involved tricks of paperwork, collusion of all parties involved, and the misplacement of lighted buoys. In 1828 the government established an admiralty court with a system of laws, licenses, and procedures to regulate the whole business. In the peak wrecking years, from 1850 until 1860, there was nearly a wreck a week on the reef, and wrecking made Key West the richest city in America. Lighthouses, updated charting of the waters, and lawyers greatly reduced this wildly profitable activity in the latter half of the century.

The military returned in 1831 upon the urging of Simonton and others who felt a military presence was critical to the security of the region. But the insects, the blazing sun, and the wild outlaw atmosphere made Lieutenant Paige and his men miserable. After pleading with Washington, Paige and his men evacuated their post in 1834. Just a year later troops returned in response to the Second Seminole War, the war of Indian resistance against white settlement and federal troops. Many of the Seminoles gave up and left along the sad Trail of Tears, but others fought on until 1842. The closest the battle got to Key West was the Indian attack on Indian Key, eighty miles up the chain of islands.

In 1845 construction of Fort Zachary Taylor began in response to threats posed by Mexico, Great Britain, and Spain. The mood in the War Department had shifted in favor of Key West once again; now viewed as critical in the security of the Gulf and the Caribbean. But again the mosquitoes, heat, and yellow fever impeded progress, and the hurricane of October 11, 1846 put a stop to everything. Most of the fort was destroyed and the lighthouse was toppled. Fifty residents were killed, and the storm surge scattered coffins and bones out of the cemetery, back into the community.

It was only a brief setback. Work on the fort and other construction resumed, the wrecking kept everyone on the lookout and busy, and sponges were discovered in the area. The sponges were plentiful, and in shallow waters local Conch spongers had only to pick them off the bottom with long-handled hooks. In the 1850s Key West was producing seventy thousand dollars worth of sponges a year, 90 percent of the sponges used in the United States.

Despite the economic boom, Key West remained a strange outpost, a decadent paradise. In 1854, one of the many yellow fever epidemics broke out, killing dozens in a long hot summer. In 1859 a fire destroyed two city blocks of downtown Key West. Fires, hurricanes, and the military were among the most consistent of Key West's visitors.

When the Civil War began, Key West, so federalized, remained with the North despite efforts by Confederates and the sentiments of locals to go along with secession. There were 400 slaves in Key West in 1850 when Walter Maloney was appointed as U.S. Marshal. Maloney, although from Georgia, was opposed to slavery and would hire only free labor for salvage work. This incensed many of the locals and tensions ran high.

Although some historians regard the occupation of Key West and The Dry Tortugas as a factor in the North's victory, a battle was never fought, a shot never fired. But the forts, Zachary Taylor on Key West and Fort

# HO! FOR KEY WEST!

## RECRUITS WANTED!
### — FOR THE PURPOSE OF
## SEIZING and HOLDING
## FORT ZACHARY TAYLOR
### IN THE NAME OF THE    UNION

The Undersigned, having been detailed on Recruiting Service by order of Captain John M. Brannan, First Artillery U.S. 1861, have opened a rendezvous in Key West, Florida, where all able bodied men can have the opportunity of enrolling their names in the annals of Glory and History by securing Fort Zachary Taylor from the grasp of treacherous secessionists, who are plotting to take control of this fortress and its guns as they have done elsewhere.

## GLORY and HONOR

For any and all men who answer this call of duty

TERM OF ENLISTMENT -

Do not miss this fine opportunity to bring a quick end to the Rebellion.

Jefferson on Garden Key at the Dry Tortugas, should be on every visitor's "A" list. You'll find details in the "What to Do" chapter, but for now a bit of Tortugas history should peak your interest.

Ponce de Leon found and named the Tortugas in 1513 for the turtles (*tortugas*) they found and slaughtered for food. The term "dry" was added when, not surprisingly, the little island was found to be lacking fresh water. The HMS Tyger wrecked there in 1742. The crew was attacked by Spaniards, but managed to survive 56 days on little Garden Key until they eventually fled to Jamaica in another 56 day ordeal. Only six men died but several, including the captain, were court-marshaled.

Construction of Fort Jefferson began in 1846; 16 million bricks on a 16 acre island. It was believed that the island sat on coral, but alas, this other ground was sinking sand. Drownings, shipwrecks, hurricanes – all proved impediments to the project and the fort was never actually finished.  In fact, it was militarily obsolete almost from the beginning. It did serve as a prison though – chiefly for Union deserters who were sent there to work. The most famous prisoner was Dr. Samuel Mudd who had set the broken leg of Lincoln's assassin, John Wilkes Booth.  Mudd arrived in 1865, tried to escape, and was put into the dungeon which you can see during your visit. Mudd worked to save the sick during a yellow fever epidemic in 1867 and was finally pardoned in 1869. The Dry Tortugas were designated as a national park in 1992.

Key West, meanwhile, was on the brink of yet another economic blessing—the arrival of cigar making. William Wall had built a cigar factory on Front

Street in the 1830s, and after the outbreak of the first Cuban War of Independence in 1868, the Ten Years' War, Vicente Martinez Ybor moved his Havana factory to Key West. E.H. Gato followed as did several other companies. U.S. tariffs against whole cigars, but not tobacco, along with the political situation in Cuba and the increasing popularity of cigar smoking in the United States (a privilege of the Gilded Age) all contributed to this flourishing industry. In the 1880s there were 100 cigar factories in Key West, employing 2000 workers. Two-thirds of the population of 18,000 was Cuban, and in 1875 Key West elected a Cuban mayor, Carlos Cespedes.

Just across the water, tensions in Cuba were rising to the breaking point. The mechanization of the sugar industry; the great gap between the haves and have-nots (slavery was not abolished until 1886); and the corrupt and inefficient colonial rule by Spain gave rise to the Cuba Libre movement centered in Key West. In 1891 Jose Marti, poet and propagandist for a free Cuba, spoke of independence from the terrace of what is now La Te Da restaurant.

Cuba finally gained its independence with the Treaty of Paris on December 10, 1898, after the sinking of the USS Maine in Havana Harbor had incited the brief and subsequent Spanish-American War. Prior to its departure to Havana, the USS Maine had been in Key West, and within a day of the explosion and sinking, the dead and wounded were returned to Key West. You can visit the dead at the special memorial in the Key West Cemetery.

In 1905 Henry Flagler began the seven year railroad construction project to connect the island to the mainland. Flagler, who had become wealthy along with Rockefeller in the building of Standard Oil, saw this as his final visionary mission. It was the sort of project that, before and since, has typified the wildly entrepreneurial but impractical dreams inflicted on Key West. The 128-mile line cost one million dollars a mile, 200 lives, and survived three hurricanes during the construction phase.

In 1912 the first train pulled into a town of 20,000 souls invested in the business of canning (turtle soup, pineapples), tourism, and cigar making, although many of the cigar factories had been lured to Tampa. An electric streetcar with five miles of track was in operation around the city. The Bijou and Monroe theaters had opened; for a dime you could see vaudeville acts as well as movies. Town leaders and the local press made efforts to curtail the drinking, gambling, cockfighting, and other wild pursuits along Duval Street, but then, as now, it was those very attractions that brought visitors from the north.

All of this was interrupted by World War One and another invasion by the military. A new air station was built in 1917, and within a year more than one thousand air cadets, instructors and sailors were on the base. The island became a training center for land and sea plane pilots, as well as blimp operators.

After the war, most of soldiers left. The cigar makers went on strike. Another hurricane hit the city on September 9, 1917; the worst yet, practically destroying the city. Key Westers took this as a wake–up call and dug in to improve the city's image as a tourist destination. They understood the need for attractions, transportation, and lodging.

In 1923 the city passed a bonding issue to build a highway from Key Largo all the way to Key West. Within two years the La Concha (at an ambitious six stories) was built on Duval, and the sprawling and lavish Casa Marina hotel went up on the southwest shore. Pan Am launched the first scheduled international passenger service from Key West to Havana; their offices were in what is now Kelly's Bar and Grill at 301 Whitehead Street. Perhaps most significantly, despite Prohibition, Key West remained a drinking town. Prohibition agents paid the occasional visit and left, understanding the situation was hopeless. Rum-running from Havana to Key West was a nightly affair and big business; weather and the Coast Guard (sometimes in the business as well), were constant threats. Key West was becoming a tourist town, but it, like the rest of the country, was suffering from increasingly hard economic times as the 20s drew to a close. Key West was a playground for the rich and famous—the haves more than the have-nots.

The famous had been coming for some time. John James Audubon came to the Keys in the 1830s, stayed in Key West in 1832. In no way a conservationist, he shot, killed, and stuffed many more birds than he painted. Still, the Audubon House on Whitehead Street is well worth a visit. Another great painter, Winslow Homer, came in the 1880s and was inspired to some of his greatest work. Zane Grey, novelist and outdoor writer for *Field and Stream* magazine, had been coming to the Keys since 1913 and was actually a conservationist, one of the first to advocate catch-and-release fishing. The actor John Barrymore came for a visit in 1924, attracted by the fishing and the booze.

The first of the major famous writers came in the 1920s. Poet and insurance executive Wallace Stevens spent much of the winter at the posh Casa Marina. He and his cronies would walk the beach, talk poetry, drink, smoke cigars, and nibble at the lavish meals served to them on the porch over-looking the Atlantic. John Dos Passos arrived in 1924 and was smitten with the gulf air, the Cuban food, the swimming, and "the calm life colored with Bacardi." It was these praises that likely influenced his friend, Ernest Hemingway, to come to Key West in the spring of 1928, just two months after the highway from the mainland had opened.

Ernest's second wife, Pauline, was seven months pregnant and they decided to rent a place on Simonton (now the gift store, Pelican Poop) to see if they liked the town enough to return after the birth of the baby. They did, of course, and the rest is history.

In the year after the Hemingway arrival, Key West suffered the same depression as the rest of the world. The population dropped by several thousand, many businesses left or closed. Neither the road, nor the railroad brought the tourists as hoped. And Prohibition ended. Unemployment was high, garbage remained uncollected, and the city itself was deep in debt. For those with money or imagination, the place remained a paradise and playground. The Hemingways went from renters to homeowners with the purchase of the place on Whitehead.

Key West was rescued from the depression by Julius Stone, a New Deal bureaucrat in Roosevelt's Federal Emergency Relief Administration. He convinced the governor to declare Key West in a state of "civil emergency." Stone enlisted 4000 local volunteers in painting fences, raking, cleaning, pulling weeds, planting gardens. He hired others to rebuild the sewer system, build a swimming pool, create ball diamonds, and clean up the beaches. Using FERA funds he furnished supplies to cottage owners who could then refurbish their bungalows themselves and rent them out to tourists. Colorful brochures, welcoming bands, theatrical productions were all part of Stone's passionate and visionary efforts.

Some of the locals, the artists and writers, the northern snow birds and long time residents were annoyed and quite vocal about this intrusion of tourism. One of the givens of Key West history is that the good times are always ending, the new arrivals ruining everything. The good times ended in bones for the Caloosas, the arrival of the Navy for the pirates, with lighthouses and regulation for the wreckers. The cigar-makers and spongers and rum-runners all faced the end of their bright prospects.

The poet Robert Frost, who had arrived with his wife in 1935, complained that the servants here felt free to sun themselves in public. And he was quite put out by Julius Stone's hairy legs. Another of Stone's crusades was the wearing of Bermuda shorts, and the short pants was the rage all over the island, quite an affront to the genteel sensibilities of Frost and his crowd. You can see the Frost cottage and Heritage House Museum at 410 Caroline.

Hemingway was annoyed by the fact that his house was number eighteen on the newly published tour guide. Other numbered highlights were the ice factory, the "typical" old house, and the aquarium with the 627 pound Jewfish. Ernest put up the brick wall you see today to keep the sightseers out. Dos Passos complained about little women on bicycles taking their book reviews to the post office; it was all too quaint, phony, and artsy.

Although lamenting the changes, Elmer Davis, a writer for the New York Times and Harper's, understood the eternal appeal of the island and commented that the "northern visitor finds that he can hold twice as much liquor and get along with half as much sleep as home." He seemed pleased that in the bars one might find "a duke, an anarchist, and a fan dancer" on adjacent barstools. This is still the case.

On September 2, 1935 the strongest hurricane ever to hit the United States roared across the middle keys with winds in excess of 200 miles per hour and a record low barometer reading of 26.35. A wall of water, higher than any point on the keys, washed over them, leaving fish scales and eels in the bent and tattered trees. The train sent down on a rescue mission was late and its timing could not have been worse. It was washed off the tracks on Matecumbe Key, just after residents and highway workers had boarded. More than 400, perhaps as many as 600 died, leaving the dead and their swollen remains in the heat of the days that followed.

Key West was barely touched by the storm, and in April of 1938 the road was fully completed without ferry breaks. In 1937 Sloppy Joe's moved, less than a block, over to Duval and Greene where it remains. Hemingway was already too infamous for his own good; he had punched the poet Wallace Stevens in the nose, had met wife number three, Martha Gelhorne, in the old Sloppy's, now Captain Tony's, then left for the Spanish Civil War. He returned briefly but was off to Cuba by 1939.

Pauline stayed behind and remained socially

active for many years, partying around with the likes of Elizabeth Bishop, the poet, and her partner Louise Crane. It is reported that the three of them enjoyed going to rumba night at Sloppy's, that Bishop, in turn, enjoyed the company of Tennessee Williams who arrived in February of 1941. Upon his arrival, they shared tea and Oreos at a brothel. Tennessee, in turn, was turned on by the sailors. And it was Williams' fame and behavior that helped establish Key West as a Gay destination.

In 1940 Count von Cosel was arrested for . . . for what exactly? It was discovered that he had kept the remains of his very young lover, Elena Milagro, nine years after her passing from tuberculosis, which he had attempted to cure with some complicated machinery of his own design. After her death, she kept falling apart. He kept moving her about town, making repairs, apparently making love to her (evidence suggests), eating meals next to her still form, applying make-up and cologne. Eventually found out, the local authorities put a stop to it. The Count was never convicted of anything, but moved north and began to feature himself as a tourist attraction. Neither love, sex, nor romance have ever been a simple matter in Key West. Elena's original grave marker is at the East Martello Museum, the whereabouts of her minimal remains, unknown.

With the start of World War II, Key West again became very busy with military activity. As the city swelled with soldiers the government claimed 2000 acres for its own. The police were overworked handling the drinking, fighting, and prostitution. The bright side of the military's investment was the water line which was establish with the mainland. The first water came down the pipe on September 22, 1942.

President Harry Truman came to Key West in 1946. He liked it so much he moved into what became known as the Little White House (the building where Thomas Edison had lived during World War I, tinkering with explosive devices for the navy), spending 175 days of his presidency here, playing poker, swimming, fishing, running the country. If you take the excellent tour of the place you'll see the famous little sign on Harry's desk: "The buck stops here."

The post-war economic boom was accompanied by the discovery of shrimp in great quantities around Key West in 1949. Millions of pounds of shrimp, "pink gold," were harvested annually by the mid 1950s. Economic growth, the efforts of The Key West Art and Historical Society, and articles in the *National Geographic* promoting the Chamber of Commerce image of the island—quaint cottages, lovely beaches, umbrella drinks, dancing and music—clashed with the eternal realties of Key West as the Mecca of sin and hedonism. *Male* magazine reported gigolos hunting for rich widows, gambling, crime, and torrid sex on the beaches, including that of lust-crazed homosexuals, regardless "of innocent onlookers." The sensationalistic reports did nothing to stop the tourists.

The Old Island Restoration Foundation was formed in 1960 for the purpose of the preservation of Old Town and the restoration of the deteriorating downtown area. Mallory Square was created, setting the stage for the nightly Sunset Celebration. And, not surprisingly, Key West attracted all of the elements of the culturally explosive decade of the 60s. Key West had reasons to feel a bit edgy anyway—located just ninety some miles from the scene of Castro's 1959 Cuban Revolution, the Bay of Pigs invasion, and the Cuban Missile Crisis of

1962. If that hadn't been enough to make city fathers nervous, the editors of the *Key West Citizen* lamented the growing numbers of homosexuals, drug users, and drifters – known as hippies.

The hippies were assimilated into the culture (Jimmy Buffett first played at Ophelia's in January of 1972), and many remain business owners in Key West. The drug dealing continues of course, but noteworthy was the big sting of 1975 when a number of major dealers were caught and convicted including five police officers, the fire chief, and the city attorney. By 1978 homosexuals were not only tolerated, gay tourism was being promoted.

Fantasy Fest started in October of 1979, part of the ever filling schedule to have something going on, some reason for coming here, at almost any time of the year: Powerboat Races (November), Pirates in Paradise Festival and New Year's Eve featuring the dropping of the drag queen on upper Duval, the dropping of the Conch at Sloppy's (December), The Key West Literary Seminar and the Sailing Races (January), Home and Garden Tours (February), Spring Break (March). The Conch Republic Independence Celebration (April), Old Island Days (May), Pridefest (June), Fishing Tournaments (Various fish – various months), Hemingway Days Festival (July), Lobster Fest (August), The Biker Bash and Poker Run (September).

In April of 1980 the Mariel boatlift took place after Castro allowed refugees to legally leave the island of Cuba. In the first two weeks 500 boats deposited 14,000 refugees on the docks of Key West, and by June 125,000 refugees had passed through processing at Truman and Trumbo annexes. Although Castro's amnesty came to an end and troops were called out to assist with the chaos, some serious fallout occurred on April 18, 1982. The Border Patrol established a roadblock on US 1 for the purpose, it was stated, to search cars coming up to the mainland for illegal aliens. They were also, it seemed, looking for other things, rifling through ice chests and glove boxes. There was a traffic jam almost 20 miles long and everyone sat in the sweltering heat for hours. Within days, the publicity caused a surge in vacation cancellations, eliciting the third call for secession and the establishment of the Conch Republic. It was decided that Key West would fire one hostile shot, surrender, and ask for billions in aid. They did and a new flag was unfurled on April 23, 1982, and the Conch Republic it remains to this day.

On Memorial Day, 1985, Mel Fisher finally found the location of the *Atocha's* incredible treasure. Much of it was under 20 feet of sand, and on July 20th, the "Big Pile," ground zero of the wreck, the largest shipwreck treasure in the world was uncovered. What had at first seemed a coral or stone reef was, in fact, a reef of silver bars. Mel Fisher's quest for the *Atocha* had lasted 16 years, had cost the lives of four people including his son, Dirk; and it took scores of court battles to win, from the government, the 450 million dollar treasure. Furthermore, the effort required the use of tubes (imagine giant leaf blowers), blasting the sea floor, creating holes and craters 20 feet down into the bottom; surely not a good thing though for the ocean and its residents.

Key West has continued to suffer under its unique allure, its position in the wide open sea and far from land, its proximity to Cuba, its attraction as a shimmering oasis on a dead end street. The AIDS Crisis and epidemic of the 1980s and 90s hit Key West just as it did Manhattan and San Francisco. Hurricanes like Wilma, the third and worst of 2005, reminded everyone, in the wake of Katrina, that the most damaging effect is not the wind but the storm surge. Wilma's winds were minimal in Key West, but the wall of water buried half the island up to its neck.

The construction of more condos and townhouses, the daily invasion of cruise ships and their credit card toting hordes, the gentrification of the island— "up scaling" every little shack, house, and parcel of "undeveloped land," actually reduces the island's lure and attraction, increases the need for fresh water and sewage disposal, and prevents the very people who work here from living anywhere nearby due to housing costs. When Cuba is open to U.S. Tourism, surely Key West will have ferry service, more visitors, and more traffic.

Perhaps eventually, if the worst of the global warming scenarios comes to pass, Key West will again sink below the surface of the sea, a little Atlantis providing structure for the fishes and corals. Even more likely, given enough somedays, just the right hurricane will blow it all away, leaving only the concrete bones of condominiums and hotels.

# 3

# *Getting Here*

People think Key West and they think Florida and they are nearly wrong. The state is comma-shaped and it's a long way from Pensacola in the panhandle to Key West at the end of the tail, 830 miles away. Key West is 160 miles southwest of Miami, about 110 miles off the mainland. And imagine this: Key West is 650 miles south of Los Angeles!

You can, of course, fly to Key West. Frequent visitors find this the best option. Major airlines fly into Miami, Orlando, Fort Meyers, Atlanta, and a few other cities, and from there you can take a smaller commuter flight down. Arriving by plane you simply take a cab to your inn, check in, take a dip in the pool if so inclined, then put on your walking shoes or pick up your bicycle and off you go. If you have mobility issues, a cab is still far better than having your own car.

The first few times I came to Key West I drove from Miami, and everyone should do that once, maybe the first time, but not if your time is limited and the focus of your vacation is Key West. Besides avoiding the hassle of the drive, if you fly into Key West, you will avoid the responsibility and expense of a car. There are more cars than parking places during busy times in Key West.

If you do plan on driving, and are coming from the Miami airport, take the Dolphin Express, Highway 836, to Florida's Turnpike, 821, then go south all the way to Florida City near Homestead. After the first few miles you will zip along, pausing occasionally to hand over dollar bills to people in the toll booths. Kids love this. If you make the mistake of taking the South Dixie Highway – US 1 – through South Miami and Coral Gables, you will creep along in exhaust fumes, past a never-ending loop of America's fifty top chain stores, and a few unsavory neighborhoods as well.

Once at Florida City, you get off the Turnpike where it ends, onto U.S. 1, then you skirt the Everglades on your way to Key Largo. The drive down US 1 is quite remarkable, truly breathtaking as you leave the mainland and start crossing the bridges. The journey is punctuated by mile markers and the countdown adds to the drama of the journey. Key Largo is at mile marker 104; then the land gradually gives way to more and more water and the bridges get longer. The longest is the seven-mile bridge stretching from Knight Key to Little Duck, mile markers 47 down to 40. The Gulf of Mexico will be on your right. The Atlantic, on your left, will glisten in the sun. Palms clatter in the breeze. Sailboats and fishing vessels dot the aqua and green water. Tiki bars appear.

There is a bit of trashiness as well; fast food restaurants, strip malls, billboards. It's tempting to stop along the way at the more alluring attractions – shell-shops, seafood restaurants, juice bars. You will see kiosks advertising discount coupons and information about Key West. These offerings are from those who wish they were actually in Key West. Keep going.

US 1 arrives on the island unceremoniously after a rather congested, beachless, and commercially unattractive last ten miles over Boca Chica and Stock Island. Once onto Key West the highway comes to a T and stoplights amidst a confusion of chain hotels and eating places. All this driving, all this money, for this? If you bear right, which makes sense, you stay on US 1 which becomes North Roosevelt Boulevard, which becomes, at the western end of the island in Old Town, Truman Avenue. Quickly, things finally look like you imagined—gingerbread houses in pink and lavender, narrow streets, giant plants, tiny lanes and tiny houses and, finally you come to Duval Street. You have arrived.

If you are one who leans towards the dramatic, for whom arrivals are filled with import and consequence; if for yourself or your passengers you'd prefer an entrance with greater promise and beauty, your heart's reward, one akin to your dreams and expectations, then take a left at the T intersection when you first come on to Key West. This will be South Roosevelt Boulevard. This route will take you along the southern side of the island with the great expanse of the Atlantic off to your left. Know that Cuba lies just over the horizon. You will pass the East Martello Tower and Museum, the entrance to the airport, and then the long and rather pretty Smathers Beach, dotted with volleyball players, vacationers of all stripes, vendors, dogs, people on bicycles. This is more the Key West you expected, and you avoid the big slump many suffer, struggling along in the heat, on North Roosevelt. You'll need to jog a bit, right on Bertha, left on Atlantic, then continue until you turn right and go north briefly on Reynolds, then left on South Street to the Southernmost Point where you'll see all the crabby people who came the other way.

Obviously, you may arrive by sea—via cruise ship, ferry services from other Florida locations, or in your own yacht. The Key West Express runs out of Marco Island and Fort Meyers and arrives at the Historic Seaport. The daily trips arrive in Key West at midday, and depart in the late afternoon. The Express now has a Miami run too for about $100 round trip. The Key West Ferry, a different outfit, departs the Miami area at Key Biscayne. Information on these services is available on websites.

Now that you're here, you need know the major streets, the districts, Old Town, New Town, where The Historic Marina or Bight Area is, and Mallory Square. Duval is just over a mile long, White Street to Fort Zachary Taylor, from the eastern to the western most limits of Old Town, is also about a mile. If you are at the Cemetery you are less than a mile from EVERYTHING. Enthusiastic walkers can do it all. But bikers can do it even better. On a bike you are no more than a leisurely 10 minutes from Fausto's Food Palace, the Sunset Celebration, and the beaches. With your gearless big-seated bike, a water bottle and sun block in your basket, you are free to explore Key West with little more effort than wishing it so.

Key West, kidney–shaped (the declivity at the top, or north), lies mostly east-west, although not quite, but close enough for discussion. The perils of navigation and orientation are due to the fact that the streets run between the compass points; they run northwest-southeast, and northeast-southwest. Furthermore, walking down (in regard to address numbers) Duval, and its important parallel neighbors, Whitehead and

Simonton, you are going northwest, not the other way. The numbering goes up as you go southeast—towards the southernmost everything. Up south, down north. And finally this: it's an island. All roads led to water and a dead-end. Navigating often requires zigzagging and a loss of orientation.

I can testify to this. Years ago, finding myself at Sloppy Joe's or thereabouts, and wanting to go to the Historic Seaport area—Schooner Wharf Bar in particular, I went up Duval to Southard and followed that to Margaret, then took a left. I knew that way because I was staying at Authors on White and Southard, and always followed Southard down to Duval for what might be found there. I also discovered, in my walks, the Historic Seaport, with a right on Margaret off Southard; and a few blocks down, there I was. But due to either the off-kilter direction of the streets, the maddening dead ends, or the darkness of night or the rum, I took a one-mile route to a destination only two blocks away, Sloppy's to the Schooner. And I did this more than once.

Some other matters of orientation: The island has no continuous perimeter road or route; the western (Old Town) half is beset with military installations, piers, bights, dead-ends and joggings, Truman Annex, and multi-story resort complexes. Only U.S. 1, also called Truman and Roosevelt, runs the length of the island towards the southwest. It crosses Duval, then Whitehead, then peters out, with mile zero at Whitehead and Petronia. Some important facts will become clear if you study the map before your arrival.

Most of what you'll see and do in Key West is bounded by Whitehead and White, the Gulf (the northwest end of Duval, near Mallory Square) and the south beaches. Most of the gaudiest night life is beheld on lower Duval, and along Greene, Front, and the boardwalk to the Historic Bight. Greene is good to know; you'll find Captain Tony's and Sloppy Joe's and it will take you to Key West Bight, the Schooner Wharf Bar, and the Conch Republic Seafood Company at the edge of the water with all the boats. If you go up (south) on Duval you'll pass the Bull and Whistle, Fat Tuesday, several retail stores, Margaretville, then, in the eight and nine hundred blocks, the gay bars, then some of the best restaurants in town—Martin's, Nine one Five, La Te Da. Here you will be among some wonderful art galleries, and further south you'll come to the Butterfly Conservatory and the Southernmost Beach Club, right on the sand.

Whitehead is rather the limit of ordinary travel in the southwestern sector of the island unless you are going through the Annex on Southard to the Fort Zachary Taylor beach and park, or are visiting Bahama village. Below Thomas is an active area of amateur drug dealing where you should not be alone, certainly not alone and drunk, especially very late at night.

Note too how you might become confused in the area of the cemetery. Some streets continue on the other side, others do not. The area around the cemetery is characterized by the tiniest lanes and tiniest houses on the island and is a great early morning biking and bird watching area.

But do venture out, even out of Old Town. South Roosevelt is a great place to watch the sun rise; East Martello Museum is on the to-do list, and Stock Island has its attractions as you will see.

Now that you know the lay of the island, you can understand why an inn in Old Town is the best choice for location. And when you set your suitcase down and send the cabbie away, you will know where you are.

*Duval is just over a mile long. At lower Duval, within a block of Sloppy Joe's at Green Street (201 Duval), you'll find Hog's Breath, Bagatelle, Captain Tony's, and The Bull and Whistle. On upper Duval you'll find the Southernmost Beach Club, the Southernmost House, and the Butterfly Conservatory at 1316 Duval.*

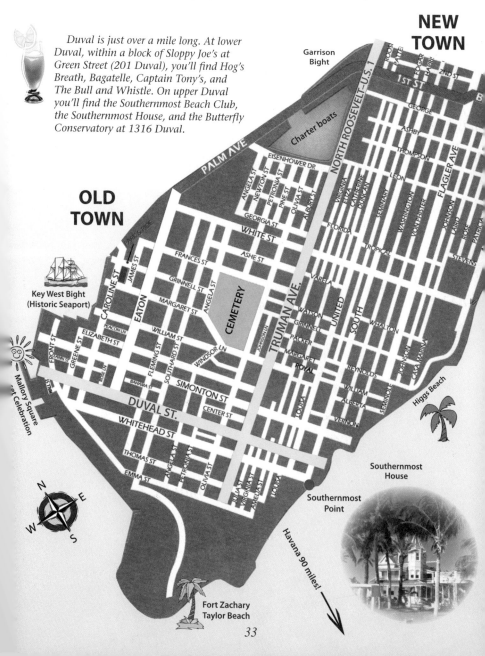

NEW TOWN

OLD TOWN

Garrison Bight

Charter boats

Key West Bight
(Historic Seaport)

CEMETERY

Mallory Square
Sunset Celebration

DUVAL ST.

WHITEHEAD ST.

Higgs Beach

Southernmost
House

Southernmost
Point

Havana 90 miles!

Fort Zachary
Taylor Beach

# 4
# Where to Stay

It's essential to book your lodgings well in advance when going to Key West. The desirable places fill up even during times of the year when you'd think this was not the case. Parrotheads in Paradise in November? Who knew? It would be rare if you could not get in somewhere, even on very short notice, but you might be staying at a chain motel on the north end, or in an $829 a night suite at the Westin, and you might not want that.

The places most in tune with the Key West experience are the beautifully restored historic inns in Old Town, many on the National Historic Register, tucked away in the lush vegetation, most with pools, some with separate cottages. These are much more than what we think of as a bed and breakfast—multistory old homes where you hear people walking on creaky floors at three in the morning, toilets flushing, bedposts rattling next door (the young couple you sat across from in the parlor at dinner).

No, we don't want that. Most of the inns have a courtyard where a continental breakfast is served, sometimes complimentary wine and cheese in the late afternoon. You can choose to schmooze, or spend most of your time away or in your room. If you are the sort who likes to hang out around a pool, do not wish to be on the go all the time, or have kids with you (some of the inns do not welcome children under 16), then choose a larger inn with some space and a bigger pool.

Just as in finding great places to eat, not all the inns are on all the websites or in the guidebooks. I will list ones I know to be good choices for reasons explained, but as you stroll the narrow streets of Old Town, or as you bike about, stop in at places that appeal to you, get their card or brochure for another time. I find these quaint and varied lodgings are interesting enough that I try to stay in a different one each time I come to Key West. On longer stays I'll switch, mid-trip. A cab driver didn't seem at all surprised one day when I loaded my suitcases into his trunk and told him to follow me (riding my bike) to the next inn. But do stay in Old Town, below White Street. It will be quiet, convenient, the perfect spot to set off on your exploration. And the stay at the inn will truly be an ongoing event.

If you just need a bed for a few hours of sleep each night, a cup of coffee and muffin in the morning, and are by yourself or with a like-minded traveler and want to save your money for a fishing trip or an all day sail, then a smaller place like **L' Habitation** might be just the thing. This tidy 1894 Conch house is small, the innkeepers friendly and out of the way, and a room will cost only $109 - $179 in any season. There is no pool, the breakfast area on the second floor back deck is a bit cramped, but the sitting porch out front is a good place to watch the traffic half a block away on Duval. The Tropic Cinema is practically next door. Almost anything you'd want to do or see is within a short walk from here. The rooms all have a private bath and refrigerator. They take well-behaved children, 12

*ockwise from upper left: the pools at
y Lime Inn, Authors, The Mermaid
d the Alligator, and Curry House.*

and older. At 408 Eaton.

You can find accommodations at the far other end of the scale four blocks away at **The Gardens Hotel** at 526 Angelina. Conde Nast has rated this place as one of the "Best in the World" for several years. The 17 rooms, cottages, and suites sit in the Peggy Mills Botanical Garden which features bricked pathways (87,000 bricks from around the world!), an aviary, ponds, fountains, a piano room, exotic plants. Peggy, a family friend of President Batista of Cuba, was here from 1930 until her death in 1979. Among her treasures from Cuba are four one ton earthenware rain collection jars. The rooms, from $300 to $680 a night, feature hardwood floors, marble baths with Jacuzzi, spa robes. No pets, no kids under 16, no surprise.

**Duval House** is very centrally located at 815 Duval, taking up much of the block actually, behind the white picket fence. The 30 rooms, among seven cottages, run from $125 to $350, with a nice room in season costing around $200 a night. The gardens are spacious, seductive, featuring Spanish lime and Banyan trees, a pool, gazebo, hammocks, and a fish pond. Parking for the car which you don't need is $11 a night. No kids under 16.

**Eden House**, owned by Mike Eden since 1975, bills itself as the oldest hotel in Key West; it was the Gibson when built in 1924. This quirky, very friendly, art-deco, gardenesque inn has a nice pool, 11 porch swings, 8 hammocks, and rooms range from $90 to $350 depending upon the season. Scott Summers wrote a short story while staying at Eden House in 1976, "Criss-Cross," and the film of the same title was filmed here with Goldie Hawn. No pets, but kid friendly.

Happy Hour, with a well-stocked bar, is complimentary from 4:00 to 5:00 daily. This is more a hotel than a bed and breakfast, and in fact, no breakfast is served. It is quietly located 5 blocks off Duval at 1015 Fleming, three blocks to the Historic Seaport.

The **Key Lime Inn** is spacious, has 37 rooms, the grounds are shady and very tranquil, and the place has one of the largest pools of any guesthouse. It's centrally located in Old Town, although it's on busy Truman Avenue (725), just down from Duval. It's one of the best places if you like to hang out and relax by a pool or in a hammock. There is free parking in the good-sized parking lot and one wonders why they made room for that. Rates range from $179 to $214.

The **Key West Bed and Breakfast** might be missed because the name of the place looks like the name of the list of places, not a place itself. It is also called The Popular House, and for good reason. It's pink, has palms out front, is small with only eight rooms, but gets rave reviews for its charm. The three-story Victorian was built by Bahamian shipbuilders and the 1898 William Russell House is listed in the National Historic Register. The rates are quite reasonable at $59 - $285. One review says that The Popular House "is what your house would look like if you had excellent taste . . . and it's a tour through the best Key West art of the past twenty-five years." At 415 William it's just a block or two from the Historic Seaport.

The **Artist House** is one of the island's Old Town supermodels at 535 Eaton. Built in the 1890s, the Colonial Queen Ann sports verandas, decorative gingerbread, and a turret. As the shadows and color, the columns, and trees, and shutters, change in the light of every hour, this is one of the most popular photo opportunities on any tour or bike ride. Gene Otto, son of the original builder and an artist, and his wife, pianist Anne (she used to play at the Rainbow Room at Rockefeller Center), lived here for many years, and the couple is buried in the cemetery with three of their Yorkies.　You might investigate the peculiar history associated with the house and the Ottos.　Gene, it seems, kept a peculiar doll, Robert, given to him when he was five, kept the doll in the turret even after he was married. The doll, apparently haunted, was blamed for some of Gene's unsavory behavior. There isn't much for grounds here, just a small wading pool, but beauty and a suspicious past will cost a little more - $120-$350.

**The Wicker Guesthouse** at 913 Duval has rooms in the main house and in cottages. Prices range from $120 to $350.　No pets, but kids are welcome.　This is a good choice for families or couples traveling together; a two-bedroom suite runs about $400. The pool is a real pool, the grounds are roomy with shaded areas, sundecks, and porches. One of the best restaurants in town, Nine-One-Five, is just next door.

**The Mermaid and the Alligator** has perhaps the most appealing sign and exterior in Key West as you come down Truman towards Duval. "Oh yes—now we're in Key West!" is what you think and feel as you pass the place, wishing it were here that you were staying. And it would be a good choice. The 1904 Queen Anne Victorian Mansion gets great reviews and wins awards for its meticulously decorated coziness. There are nine suites and rooms, the rates ranging from $218 to $298. The rooms have themes: bamboo, garden, Audubon, papaya. There is a plunge  pool with benches and jets, and more than a continental breakfast.  No guests under

16, and no pets, although your hosts, in addition to Dean and Paul, include one or more friendly resident dogs.

**Cypress House** complex includes the Simonton House and the Cypress House Studios, comprising a total of 26 rooms based at 601 Caroline. The Cypress House itself is another Bahamian Conch mansion, built in 1888 and is listed on the National Register. There is a big pool, beautiful gardens, a complimentary cocktail hour from 6:00 until 7:00 with a full bar. The breakfast buffet is far beyond the common continental offering. The front of Cypress is weathered wood with colorful flags, a very recognizable Key West landmark. The place is richly Key West and the rooms are appropriately priced at $159 - $430. A bit more for a suite in high season. The inn requires a five day minimum stay during the winter season (December through April), a seven day minimum for Fantasy Fest and New Years. This seems a bit restrictive, and this inn has the longest minimum stay requirements that I could find. Shoulder seasons require a three day minimum.

**Heron House** is lush, upscale, has a nice pool and 23 wonderfully appointed rooms—stained glass, fine woodwork, meticulously decorated. The gardens feature orchids and over 1000 (so say the owners) exotic plants. It's at 512 Simonton, just off Fleming. The rates start at $200-$300, but still a good value for the money and location. It's another good choice for romance and tropical luxury along with The Gardens Hotel.

I've stayed at **Authors** several times. The quarters are a bit tight, a main house and two cottages. The pool is tiny but certainly refreshing, and the rates reasonable. Some of the smaller rooms go for under $100. Also, there is the name of the place which attracts, surely, the bookish set. The ten rooms and cottages are named after Key West authors—Carson McCullers, Thornton Wilder, Tennessee Williams. It's at 725 White Street, a quiet neighborhood, away from all the buzz. Children are welcome, but not pets or Spring Breakers. Breakers break things.

**Curry House** and Curry Mansion are very different places. Curry House at 806 Fleming is a house with nine rooms, two with a shared bath. It has a great pool and a terrific hot breakfast—bacon and eggs, French toast, something different every morning; and one of the most generous wine bars in the late afternoon. The late afternoons often find guests in easy conversation around the pool at Curry House; the magic of wine! The rates range from $109 to $259. No pets, no kids under 13.

The **Curry Mansion** is just off Duval at 511 Caroline. A real 1899 Mansion, construction was first begun by William Curry, Key West's first millionaire. It's very upscale, lush, with a nice pool area, and a small museum in its own right. Key lime pie was invented here. If you visit, go all the way up through the attic to the widow's walk (wives awaiting overdue sailor husbands came to these rooftop decks to search the horizon for homebound sails). The 22 rooms run from $195 to $365. They offer parking, a full breakfast, and a cocktail hour.

The **Banyan Guesthouse** at 323 Whitehead, will set you back $250-$400 a night in season. Since it's a time-share operation it also seems difficult to book, but try if you can afford it. It's got a tiki bar, two heated pools, and is set in lush gardens amidst giant (and continually photographed from the street) Banyan trees.

**La Mer Hotel and Dewey House** are part of the Southernmost complex that also includes the **Southernmost Hotel** and **Southernmost On the Beach**—that part of the hotel right on the water with a very large pool. The Southernmost Hotel—yes it's hard to keep them all straight—is across the street, inland, and is a sprawling, regular-but-nice sort of place with two pools, a tiki bar, travel services, all that. You can get a room here for under $200. The Inns—Dewey House (former home of philosopher John Dewey), and La Mer Hotel (adjacent—they are connected by the garden) are in the luxury class. When they advertise boutique rooms with private patios, Jacuzzis, robes, turndown service, a deluxe breakfast and afternoon tea, you know you will be paying $300-$400 and up for a garden or ocean view room. You have beach and resort privileges at the other properties in the group. It truly is deluxe here; the ocean right at your feet with its changing colors and breeze. But the whole complex has a busy, corporate resort kind of feeling, like an all-inclusive. I sometimes bike here, lock the bike in a rack, get an ice cream cone or have a drink at the Southernmost Beach Club, watch the comings and goings, then bike away.

**Angelina Guest House**, at 302 Angelina, advertises no phones and no TV, accepts no guests under 18, and is another of those quiet Old Town guesthouses that seem far away from the Southernmost complex in so many ways. This former 1920s bordello has tasteful rooms in the $69-$179 range, the lower prices for a shared bath in the off-season. The smallest rooms are a bit bare and square, but remember that these were rooms with a function; you and your significant other might like to role play. Afterwards, swim in the very nice pool, then fall asleep in a hammock listening to the little waterfall. The continental breakfast includes homemade cinnamon rolls, but if that's not enough, Blue Heaven, a block away, features the most memorable breakfast in town.

Although many Key West inns are gay friendly, a few are gay exclusive: **Island House**, **Coral Tree Inn**, **Oasis**, and **Coconut Grove** are all men only. **Pearl's Rainbow** offers 38 rooms for women only. Straight people needn't worry about stumbling in to one of these places unintentionally; they are very upfront in their marketing and on initial contact as to what they offer.

There are many fine, large luxury hotels on the water in Old Town: **Ocean Key Resort and Spa**, **Pier House**, **The Westin** (about this place, adjacent to Mallory Square and now surrounding The Customs House, Joy Williams wrote, "Wandering around this brick-pavilioned complex, one feels close to resembling a stick figure in an architectural drawing."). Rates at the Westin run from $299 to $949. The historic **La Concha**, not on the water, is right on Duval. At **The Top**, the rooftop bar, you can survey the city and watch the sunset, perhaps catch the green flash as the sun's upper rim sinks into the sea. Down on the south end of Old Town the grand and very famous **Casa Marina** sits on 1000 feet of beach and advertises more than 300 rooms. Lou Gehrig stayed in one once, says one blurb. The place is huge, sprawling, a tropical Grand Hotel with tennis courts and several bars. It's very expensive but kids under 19 stay free. There are a few moderately priced "regular" motels inland in Old Town, generally in the area of Duval and Truman and to the south—

**El Patio**, **El Rancho**, and the **Ocean Breeze Inn**. And finally, on the north end, in the busy-yet-far-away-from-everything you'll find other chain hotels— **Comfort Inn**, **Holiday Inn**, and **Days Inn**. These may have an ocean view and a pool, but they are not really in Key West.

*Upper right: The tasteful ambience of the former bordello in the hall at Angelina House; all others—Key West Bed and Breakfast.*

This is RED FISH BLUE FISH

A & B
Lobster House
RESTAURANT

PISCES
A SEAFOOD PLACE

# 5

## *Eating*

In a city of appetites it is all too easy to grab a bite when you are hungry, rushed, and on the way to somewhere else. You might order a greasy basket of something, an ice cream cone, a slice of pizza, or a street dog, not only blowing your pledge of moderation (not a good idea here anyway) but spoiling an opportunity to eat something new or wonderful while sitting in a garden or watching the ships come in. Key West has a remarkable variety of eating establishments and eating should not be haphazard. It should be a main event. And surely you didn't come all this way to spend your money at Denny's, Friday's, Outback, Hard Rock, or at Kentucky Fried.

Be aware that the various Key West dining guides consist of paid-for listings. The latest edition of *The Menu*, for example, does not list Antonia's, Banana Café, Blue Heaven, Louie's Backyard, Mangia Mangia, Mangoes, Nine One Five, or Square One—eight of, perhaps, the best fifteen restaurants in town. But it does list IHOP. And Margit Bisztray's excellent *The Complete Key West Dining Guide* does not discuss Bagatelle, The Rooftop, or Mangoes, but it is literature: "Several specialties play with degrees of cooking, such as the rigatoni with sautéed shrimp, prosciutto, garlic, barely melted tomatoes, dried pepper flakes and a handful of radicchio, arugula, and Belgian endive on top, adding a raw bite for the final punctuation." That's from her entry for Mangia Mangia. This is from the write-up of Hot Tin Roof: "Salads look groomed for show, including one with mixed greens, mango, papaya, rum-soaked red onions, and a frisky passion fruit vinaigrette." This is a writer's town and writing is everywhere.

Back home, in northern Minnesota, dinner out features large portions, a trip to the salad bar (corn relish, liver pate, potato salad, iceberg lettuce, croutons, beet slices, French or Italian dressing), a roll, coffee—and a bill of about $15.00. I am both a bit naïve and suspicious of food writing that goes on and on about who does the better reduction, has the most elegant vegetables, who reigns as the most innovative chef in town. It seems to me that one's dining companions, the weather, what you are drinking, the luck of your selection, along with the comfort of your chair and the proximity of other attractive and interesting diners have more to do with your good time and estimation of the food than anything else.

Since it is the first concern of the day, and sometimes problematic, we will start with breakfast. Many restaurants do not serve breakfast, some that do open later than convenient, and it is the meal where a person's compulsivity is most clearly focused: "Eggs over easy, yolks liquid but not broken, on wheat toast with no butter."

**Blue Heaven**; and heaven it is. Although you can get any of the day's meals here, it's best for breakfast, in the early cool of the day, beneath the giant shade trees, mindful of Hemingway's time in the back yard, its history as a brothel, a place for gambling, cockfights and boxing decades ago. There are also noisy roosters, no better accompaniment to your lobster omelet. The specialty pancakes, home made granola, funky wait staff, and the cat and rooster gravestones over in the corner make this spot the essence of a Key West morning. It's also perfectly located to start an efficient day's tour. Eat here early, walk or bike two blocks to Hemingway's House for the tour; you are then quite close to the Key West Lighthouse where you can get the best bird's eye view of the island.

**The Rooftop Cafe** – is on Front Street, amidst the treetops, at the center of downtown Old Town. When I first came to Key West I had breakfast here almost every morning, despite the drive from my chain motel in New Town. A thawing northern Minnesotan, I couldn't quite grasp eating outside, on a deck, in the morning hours of January when back home the temperature was, in fact, 100 degrees colder. I would write out postcards here, talk about the bird sounds, the roosters, the scent of the briny ocean while eating my tree house (or lobster Benedict) omelet, or granola and yogurt with fruit. I have brought friends here for late dinners, for the romantic atmosphere, the great food, the music (piano bar, jazz) and the odd things that frequently occur. Once, after a wonderful meal under the warm tropical stars, a drag queen clattered up the stairs, asked the piano player for "Danny Boy," then began belting out the song. Then he asked for another song, then took a man who was seated with his wife up into his arms and whirled him around the floor, dancing. This man, who looked like a retired accountant from Iowa, seemed to enjoy the dance, and the beaming wife didn't mind sitting this one out. We all enjoyed ourselves. This has never happened where I live. Breakfast isn't available here until 9:30; best for one of your lazy mornings

**Harpoon Harry's** is on Caroline near the Historic Seaport, opens very early, is inexpensive, long-famous, where lots of locals (fisherman, boat crews) eat their bacon and eggs and toast. It's bustling, noisy with conversation, the daily special sliding out of the kitchen with great regularity. You can eat at the counter or in a booth and your coffee cup is always full. It feels like 1965 here.

**Pepe's**, advertising itself as the oldest eating establishment on the island (since 1919), is just down the street from Harpoon Harry's. It's weathered, cozy, another one-of-a-kind and the kind of place that is disappearing. A huge painting of a nude woman hangs inside where the ceiling fan slowly turns; or you can eat out on in the courtyard under the awnings amidst the foliage. No chickens.

Up at the south end of downtown, at Simonton and Catherine, is **Camille's** on the site of the old Blue Moon Café where Phillip Caputo's 569 pound marlin used to hang. Nobody seems to know where the fish is now. Camille's used to be on Duval, was much smaller, and you had to wait in line. This place is much bigger, perhaps less famous than it used to be, but everybody still raves about the food, breakfast certainly.

According to your mood and location you will also enjoy **Croissants de France** at 816 Duval. It's both very French and very Key West with patio seating. It opens at 7:30, serving eggs—brioches and benedicts—and French Toast, croissants, crepes, and beignets. They also make the very rare galettes, buckwheat crepes.

Lunch is served anytime after 9:00—soups, quiches, sandwiches. This is also a chocolaterie. Imagine a warm January morning, seated on a deck under the trees, roosters and doves in distant conversation, France in Key West; you are so not in Kansas anymore.

Up the street at 1211 Duval is another French place, **Banana Café**. You can eat in the cute little house or outside. They open at 8:00 for breakfast and will make lunch for you anytime until closing at 4:00 P.M. Among the great omelets is one with Norwegian salmon, sour cream, and caramelized onions. And under crepes you'll find one with goat cheese, walnuts, and caramelized apples.

**Sarabeth's** is related to the New York Sarabeth's, right in the middle of Old Town at 530 Simonton. This neighborhood restaurant gets top reviews from everybody and is truly a must eatery. "The best I've ever had!" is often in response to the crab cakes, muffins and fruit toppings, tomato soup, burgers, and French Toast. Their Four Flowers juice is a mix of orange, pomegranate, banana, and pineapple juices. Have that, then the Goldie Lox. Excellent atmosphere, great staff. There is a reason so many locals take their guests here. Dinners and lunches are excellent as well.

And speaking of lunch, **BO's Fish Wagon** was once just a wagon, but for years now it's been a shack on the corner at 801 Caroline. This is a walk up; funky old traditional Key West. They take your name and order and come out several minutes later with some of the best, freshest, tastiest "fast food" you've ever eaten. The fish sandwich or the scallops, deep-fried or grilled, along with some fries and a cold beer will put a song in your sun burned heart.

**Hogfish Bar and Grill** over on Stock Island advertises itself as "a great place if you can find it." The map shows Maloney as a right off U.S. 1 coming from Key West, but it's really MacDonald which quickly turns into Maloney. Turn right on 4th Avenue, inconspicuous and easy to miss but across from Boyd's Camp. Then, you'll note that a quick left on Front Street is required. Front is just a hundred feet or so from Maloney and the sign is behind some junk or a trailer or something and that is why I failed to find Hogfish on my second and third attempts (I was foiled by the MacDonald-Maloney mix-up the first time). I finally found Hogfish on the fourth try, amidst junkyards, post-apocalyptic debris, in a setting that looks right out of *The Night of The Living Dead* movies. But it was worth it all. It's a real sailors' and pirates' redneck and hippie kind of place where you can get something you can't get, hardly, anywhere else: The World Famous "Killer" Hogfish Sandwich with onions and mushrooms on fresh baked Cuban bread.

**The Turtle Kraals Restaurant & Bar**: This is a

good place to eat at the bar, especially if you are eating alone, a place with a decidedly informal atmosphere (the tourists seem to have cheerfully stumbled upon the place). Shorts, tank top, and flip flops are the dress code. Fishermen and other locals eat and drink here. It's just down the boardwalk from Schooner Wharf Bar. Both are right on the water in the Historic Harbor District. Gulls and pelicans hang out, tarpon and other fish cruise along below the boardwalk. There is a briny scent, fishy even, in the air, and much bustling about the schooners and yachts, the dinghies and flats boats.

Turtle Kraals is not really cuisine, not fine dining, but the daily specials posted on the chalkboard are truly special, and usually include a catch or two of the day – blackened, grilled, fried, or encrusted with something, served with vegetables and toast. The beer list is extensive. You'll rarely spend over $20 for an entrée. This is the place to come upon your arrival in town when you're still edgy and frazzled. You'll feel rather at home, anonymous over your beans and rice and lobster, the cold beer going quickly to your head.

I once attended a writing workshop with former United States Poet Laureate Billy Collins as the instructor. When we concluded our final session at the Pier House, our little group, still basking in the glow of the most popular poet since Robert Frost, decided to go out for a drink and lunch at the Turtle Kraals. At the end of the meal Billy asked me how I liked my grouper (we had both ordered the encrusted grouper special, both of us drank two Amber Bock). "Oh, it's excellent," I said. Billy thought so too. Although lunching with Billy Collins was the literary equivalent of a devout Catholic lunching with the Pope, Turtle Kraals was a favorite of mine even before that.

**Salute** is on Atlantic Boulevard near Higg's Beach. This is a wildly colorful, mostly open-air place with a Mexican beach feel to it – maybe it's the sand, the palms, the water, its isolation from the usual Key West buzz, hustle, and weirdness. A good spot for an iced tea and a mahi salad if you've spent time at Smather's Beach, or if the afternoon heat is a bit much during your bike ride.

For dinner, **Bagatelle** is a good choice for first time visitors. For some reason it does not appear in many of the guides (they are so busy, perhaps they don't need the exposure, or the expense), but the food is great, the drinks Key West spectacular, and the people watching couldn't be better. For me, it is quintessential, in your face Key West. Much of the seating is on the outdoor porches—upstairs and down—at this beautiful old Victorian Mansion. It was originally called the Rose Tattoo and Tennessee Williams himself was a regular in the 1970s. In those same years, his plays—*Cat on a Hot Tin Roof, The Glass Menagerie*—were staged just down the street and around the corner at the Waterfront Playhouse. It is at 115 Duval, ground zero for downtown action, just a few blocks from Mallory Square, Sloppy Joe's, Captain Tony's, the ocean, the music.

**Pisces** at 1007 Simonton is the renamed and "evolved" Cafe Des Artistes. It is a boutique restaurant with boutique prices. A small historical note provides another Key West story: The building dates from 1892 when it was a tin wares store, later a home for cigar maker Ignacio Castillano; then, in 1937, The Gulf Stream, a restaurant and hotel operated by Al Capone's bookkeeper. That soon failed, giving way to other ventures until Café des Artistes was created in 1983 by current owner Timothy Ryan. The décor features signed Andy Warhol prints.  The wine list is sophisticated.  Pisces Aphrodite is an appetizer—fruits of the sea in pastry.  The long-time signature dish of the restaurant is Lobster Tango Mango.  The appetizer Roulade "Czarina" brings evocative menu writing to the brink: "Smoked Salmon and Goat Cheese wrapped in Crisp Potato with Horseradish Crème Fraiche, Pickled Beets and Cucumber."

**Michaels** is another of the three or four restaurants regarded as the best in town, especially if you like steak. Its Filet al Forno—tenderloin rubbed in garlic and Roquefort—has won awards.  The place is also known for the veal chop, fondue, duck, the stuffed grouper, and a dessert, The Chocolate Volcano. As befits a steak place they serve a variety of great martinis and have a serious wine list. Michaels is romantic, out of the way, and expensive—at 535 Margaret.

**Louie's Backyard** is most often regarded as Key West's favorite restaurant. It's in a beautiful old mansion right on the beach, the food is remarkable, and as for

the atmosphere, Bisztray's dining guide points out that food writers often list this "as one of the world's most gorgeous restaurants." This is one of the few places in Key West where, while dining or drinking, you can hear the waves breaking on the shore, small hissing waves, waves accompanying an Atlantic moon, or distant sails filled with the wind, Havana just over the curve of the earth. Have the lobster, shrimp, lamb, yellowfin tuna, or the roast breast and braised leg of duck with red wine, ginger, and figs. Lunch is served 11:30 – 3:00, dinner 6:00 – 10:30. The Afterdeck Bar stays open until 1:00 a.m.

**Mangia Mangia**: This is the site of the best pasta experience of my life. It was veal in alfredo sauce with mushrooms, and when I bit into the first tender noodle there was an explosion that set off a sensation of amber waves of grain, walnuts, feed sacks, the purity of soil and weather. I was alone at my table, eating so slowly that the waiter asked me if everything was all right. I said it was more than all right, I said this was one of the best things I'd ever tasted and I didn't want it to end. He walked away, probably thinking I'd had too much to drink, was sentimental or lonely; I'd actually only just started on my Super Tuscan, quite memorable as well. The wine list here is said to be the best in town. The waiter checked back just once more. This is one of those "recommended by locals" sort of places in a quiet residential neighborhood – like Sole, or Michael's —that will really round out and legitimize your trip to Key West.

**Nine One Five** is at, logically, 915 Duval. Like Bagatelle, this is in a restored Victorian mansion where you can eat upstairs or down, inside or out, on one of the porches, but this place is quieter, informal, yet a bit exotic, the first choice for many locals and frequent visitors to Key West. You will remember the Thai whole fish in sizzling chili garlic sauce and steamed Basmati rice, or the Dungeness crab wrapped with Ahi tuna for a very long time. And the prices are reasonable—an entrée will rarely cost you more than $30.

A local, a world traveling gourmand, or any other writer might come up with a list quite different from this one, but most would include the majority of the eating places I've discussed. You'll hear about the following, all worthy of your discovery: Santiago's Bodega, El Sibony, the coffee and sandwiches at Five Brother's Grocery (all Cuban), the sushi at Origami, the Italian at La Trattoria or Antonia's (Leonard Bernstein's favorite) lunch at Mangoes on busy Duval where, it is said, Hillary likes to go, surely Alice's (another Key West tradition), and Marquesa, Square One (fancy, pricey, but spectacular food and service), Café Sole, Martin's, and Kelly's Caribbean Bar and Grill at the site of the original Pan Am office.

# 6
## *Drinking*

Key West floats as much in alcohol as it does in salt water. It's hot. People don't keep regular hours. There is a sense of permission here. One popular t-shirt proclaims that "AA Is for Quitters," another "The Liver Is Evil and Must Be Punished!" Responsibilities are minimal, and the island spawns longings for immortality that call for a drink: a cold beer, the ubiquitous pina colada, mai tai or margarita, as well as libations tied to the island itself and its diverse history and culture: the rum runner, Cuba Libre, mojito, key lime martini, and the Sloppy Rita. It may seem that everyone is drinking all the time and everywhere. A wonderful party it is. But those staying longer than a few days are wise to notice that these are not the same people drinking everywhere and all the time. The cast changes continually and you should be among those. And be aware that Key West is so odd and off kilter that it's hard to know if you are drunk or not. Chickens pass beneath your breakfast table. A dog stands at the corner with a cat perched on his back, and on the cat stands a little gray mouse. Here is a wizard, there a drag queen. If you come from the frozen north, the very trees, flowers, the air itself seem like special effects. At sunset, hundreds of people stare into the sun as it sinks into the gulf. How is one to know sobriety?

And you don't want to ruin a short trip, or any trip, with giant or frequent hangovers. Hemingway said something to the effect that the trick is to not drink so much that it ruins your liver and prevents more drinking. We could draw from this observation to say that you should not drink so much in Key West as to prevent more of experiencing, and drinking in, Key West. This is quite important to remember if you have an aquatic adventure planned for the next day. You don't want to feed the fishes with last night's indiscretion.

Key West has an open container law but they don't seem to enforce it if you're just crossing the street to another bar, or if you're standing outside the place where you bought the drink, catching some air or watching the girls watching the boys watching the boys and girls. But if you misbehave—try to start your Moped, pinch the nice man's wife, or pee within sight of 200 people—you may very well be jailed for, if nothing else, the open container.

Pirates, limes, rum, Cuban sugarcane just over the horizon—no wonder certain drinks feature these ingredients and influences. Limes open our minds and taste buds to the wondrous flavors at hand. Rum keeps us mindful of the brave sailors of Prohibition who kept the party going in the 1920s. The Cuba Libre (rum, cola, lime) is best offered as a toast to Jose Marti at La Te Da. If you order a round of mojitoes, remember to tip your bartender something extra as these are very labor intensive, requiring fresh crushed mint along with sugar, rum, lime juice, and club soda. Try the Pirate's Punch at Captain Tony's. The recipe is a secret; if you ask the bartender what's in it, he'll answer, "Why Honey, just pure goodness!"

Most places feature a key lime martini which is
sometimes quite good, sometimes not. Beer is really the
drink of the island. It's hot, people have a thirst which,
given the amount of fluid required, is best quenched
by drinking something with less alcohol than wine or
rum. Early in the morning, just after dawn, after a still
and rainless night, lower Duval smells strongly of beer,
beer warming on the pavement, beer amidst the broken
glass on the sidewalks, and when the garbage trucks
come down the street and pick up the dumpsters, you
can hear the rolling boom and tinkle of beer bottles,
thousands of them, from blocks away.

Drinkers probably require less assistance than anyone
else in finding what they want. Yet, here we are, aren't
we? In addition to the information that follows on some
very important bars, you may find **Key West Bar Tab**
quite useful and amusing. The pocket-sized monthly
features music schedules, happy hour specials, clever
interviews and profiles, and miscellaneous trivia.

**Captain Tony's**, half a block from Sloppy's at 428
Greene, is the oldest licensed saloon in Florida. It is
dark, a bit musty, cave-like, and filled with ghosts. The
ceiling is festooned with brassieres, the walls thickly
layered with decades old business cards. In the 1800s
the building was an ice house, the city morgue, and
a telegraph station. News of the sinking of the USS
*Maine* was sent out from within these walls. It was, for
a time, a cigar factory, a bordello, and a speakeasy. Josie
Russell bought the place in 1933; it was the original
Sloppy Joe's and Ernest Hemingway's hangout most
afternoons until 1938 when Josie moved the place over
to Duval (the current Sloppy's), and Ernest left for Cuba
and elsewhere with Martha Gelhorn whom he met here
over drinks in 1936. The bar became the Duval Club, a

gay bar, in 1940. Captain Tony Tarracino (See Captain in the Glossary) bought the place in 1958 and Captain Tony's it remains. It's stools have been graced with the weight of Jimmy Buffett, Tennessee Williams, Truman Capote, Harry Truman, and Liz Taylor.

**Sloppy Joe's** is ground zero at Greene and Duval. From late morning until early morning the tourists come and go, the booze flows, the bands play on—adult musical comedy, oldies, rock and roll, blues piano; noon until 2:00 a.m. Then you have two hours to finish drinking. This is the number one stop for freshly arrived snowbirds in the winter, wildly festive people from Michigan and Ohio and Indiana losing their grip on reality about the time they would be tuning in to Letterman. The bar food is the greasy-in-a-basket variety. The bouncers are very earnest. The souvenir shop adjacent will sell you everything from coasters and caps to sweatshirts and tanks, all with the Nobel Prize winner looking back at you.

**Green Parrot** at Whitehead and Southard is a long-time institution and is a locals' favorite. "See the Keys on your hands and knees!" is one of their shirt's logos, but this is more than a tourist joint and the place rocks. Often the best music in town is found here; they draw groups from all over the U.S. and feature rhythm and blues, rock, honky-tonk, funk and the place overflows into the street when the band is good. This is a serious bar: smokers, bikers, guys wearing caps. No sniveling. No cover, no minimum, no wonder.

At Pier House there is the **Chart Room**. It's behind the pool on the inland side of the courtyard, hidden by the dense foliage. No blender drinks here—small, dark, the kind of bar in which you might want to wait out a hurricane. It's a masculine, serious kind of bar, with the reputation that extremely famous people can be seen in its small confines. I've come here for the generous and well made martini, feeling a bit famous myself afterward.

**Schooner Wharf Bar** on the boardwalk at the Key West Bight is regarded as the best of the real, old Key West. It hangs at the edge of the water, only steps away from where you might disembark your afternoon snorkel boat. The live music here includes rock, folk, and naughty sea songs. Buy a fresh cigar at the kiosk, read the lewd graffiti in the cramped bathroom, order a dozen raw oysters on the half shell.

The **Conch Republic Seafood Company** is on the water at the end of Green Street, within sight of the Schooner Wharf Bar. It has the longest bar on the island and features 80 rums from around the world. They offer award-winning appetizers. The two-for-one happy hour draws a large and festive crowd.

**Margaritaville:** No, it's not hard to get in, quite easy most of the time actually. They have decent bar food, good music, but the place seems to lack magic for whatever reason. Yet loads of cruise boat people and new tourists in town come here, have a drink and eat a cheeseburger, then go after the Parrothead stuff in the adjacent store before moving on.

**Hog's Breath** is home to another famous Key West slogan: "Hogs Breath—Better than no breath at all!" Just down a block from Sloppy's, this place, like Green Parrott, features excellent music from 1:00 P.M. until 2:00 A.M. daily. It's partly outside and under the trees.

**801 Bourbon**—at 801 Duval—and **Bourbon Street**, up at 724 Duval are two of the gay bars in a three block stretch with others. They feature TV porn, dancing on the bars, drag shows. Surely, nimble septuagenarians from Ohio or Utah have walked this far from their cruise ship, only to have the bejesus scared out of them.

**The Bull and Whistle** is a barn-like, dark, drafty saloon at Duval and Caroline. Elvis appears there in the afternoons, a lure to the cruise ship folks. The big open windows on the ground level and the open balcony upstairs provide good street viewing. If you go up one more flight of stairs to the bar on the roof, you'll find naked people. The bar has an old time saloon atmosphere, popular drink specials, and you can hear the rock and roll at night for blocks.

**Jack Flats**, with its fishing theme at 509 Duval, has seven TV screens, darts, pool, and shuffleboard. It's like your best sports bar back home; busy, noisy, youthful, straight. If you've had too much of Key West, feel the place is way too odd for your mainstream sensibilitites, take refuge here.

**Virgilio's** at 524 Duval, behind La Trattoria, is a classy martini bar with live jazz, Salsa, and other music three or four nights a week. This patio bar is a nice romantic hideaway.

**Louie's Afterdeck Bar,** also discussed under places to eat, is the perfect spot for outdoor drinking under the full moon and stars. The best place for a mojito.

**Grand Vin Wine Bar** at 1107 Duval is a quiet late afternoon place to hang out and enjoy a flight of whatever they are pouring. Informal, informative, and friendly—a great selection for take-home as well. You

can watch the world stroll by on the sidewalk.

There is a bar for every thirst and notion in Key West. You can eat an eighteen ounce rib-eye, or ride the mechanical bull at **Cowboy Bill's Honky Tonk** at 610 Duval. You can get anything frozen, and a big headache, at **Fat Tuesday**.

**The Lost Weekend Liquor Store** is a little hole in the wall just behind The Bull and Whistle on Caroline. This package store's name will be lost on spring breakers, anyone younger than the older baby boomers. *The Lost Weekend*, released in 1945, starred Ray Milland and Jane Wyman and chronicled the grotesque binge of a disintegrating failed and alcoholic writer. The score of the film features excerpts from *La Traviata*. Many a would-be writer has come to Key West, only to be lost forever in the bars. If this store's name is meant to suggest the object lesson, it has gone unheeded.

Know this: In Key West, more than in any other place, some of us drink because we are poets, the rest of us because we are not.

Michael McCloud at The Schooner Wharf Bar

*A bicycle is your key to freedom in Key West.*

# 7
# *What to Do*

So what does one do in Key West, given a few days? What is it that cannot be done at home? What should be the take-home lesson, the experience which will remain unforgettable? Each visitor is unique, and there are many Key Wests. Here are the keys to some of them.

**Walking and Biking**—The very best way to experience Key West is on foot or with a bike; your senses and whims lead you to discovery at your own pace. The nooks and crannies are infinite and each day is a different season. The advantage of renting a bicycle is that you can cover more ground if your days are limited. In Old Town a bike is as fast as a car; you can park and lock it anywhere, it's cheap, and there is something about the breeze in your face, the scent of the flowers, the passing faces and sights and sounds that is like a terrific personal travelogue on every ride. A bike is the best way to see and do most things in this book; you can stop, look, park, or move on. And once you get a bit of a tan and have a bag of groceries from Fausto's Food Palace in your basket, you will look and feel like a local. And you're getting some exercise, burning off last night's cuisine. A bike is the perfect way to go to the beach (and at Fort Zach you save the car fee), the Sunset Celebration, and the best way to see early-morning Key West—when the roosters are crowing; when you can see the sunrise out on Atlantic or South Roosevelt Boulevard; when the new air has come in off the ocean; and when, for a little while, the city seems washed and clean.

It should cost you no more than $40 to $50 to rent a bike for one week, no more than $12 for 24 hours. Make sure the seat is adjusted, the tires are inflated properly, the lights work, and that you know how to operate the lock and cable before you leave the shop. **Moped Hospital** at 601 Truman and **The Bicycle Center** at 523 Truman have a good supply of bikes and provide helpful, friendly service. **Bike Rentals Key West** will deliver the bike to your inn and provide road-side service, as will **Eaton Bikes**.

Whether biking or walking, pick up Sharon Wells' *Walking and Biking Guide*. This is one of the most useful publications on the island. It has detailed maps and descriptions of whatever you might want to see —historic homes and neighborhoods, the art galleries, nature treks, the Gay Trek, the Cemetery, the Historic Seaport, Downtown and Mallory Square, and Duval Street.

An early morning self-guided tour of the **Key West Cemetery**, on foot or on a bike, is the perfect antidote to a night of drinking. It will be quiet and cool and the dead will remind you, along with your headache, of your final end. You will be contemplative, reflective, most in tune with the departed, most susceptible to turning your life around. Here you will find victims of murder and suicide, death by dynamite, men who went down with the *USS Maine*. Buried here are the

remains of a famous midget, a deer, dogs, and Sloppy Joe Russell. Guided walking tours are advertised, but you can do the tour just as well and at your own pace with the brochure and map available at the entrance to the cemetery. The map will help you find everything: Where are the Jews? The Catholics? The midget? The printed guide reveals the meaning of gravestone symbols (oak leaves = strength, the lily = chastity). You've heard that one gravestone reads, "I told you I was sick." My favorites are, "I'm just resting my eyes," and "Devoted Fan of Singer Julio Iglesias."

Although Hemingway was a bad boy, a man of his time in so many ways—arrogant boozer, misogynist, hunter, fisherman, aficionado of the bullfight—his writing, powerfully evocative, has stood the test of time. And his ghost here, attracting visitors literary or not, remains a powerful influence on the island. How else to explain all the middle aged men smoking cigars down at Mallory Square, staring wistfully out towards the Gulf Stream?

Even if you are not a fan of Hemingway or his work, a visit to **Hemingway House** is a requirement. You'll learn about the construction of the house, built from mined coral, by shipper and wrecker Asa Tift in 1851; how and why the house has one of the few basements, and one of the first pools in the city. You'll see a Spanish birthing chair, Mexican and Italian antiques, a china figurine given to Ernest by Marlene Dietrich, the writing room (separated from the main house by a rope bridge when the writer was there) where Hemingway wrote *Death in the Afternoon, To Have and to Have Not,* and much of his best work. In the house and on the spacious grounds you'll catch a whiff of history, maybe feel the hairs on the back of your neck stand up.

Like the other tours, see Hemingway House in the morning to avoid the crowds and heat, and do take the guided tour—it's optional but the guides are very informative and entertaining. Then hang out, take a few pictures, linger on the porch, buy a book or two in the bookstore. Later, in your hammock, sip a Papa Doble, puff on a cigar, read to your fellow travelers something from *The Old Man and the Sea,* then offer up a toast to the old bastard.

**The Lighthouse Museum** is across the street

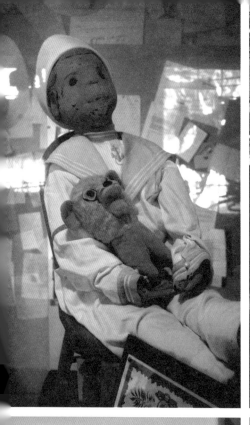

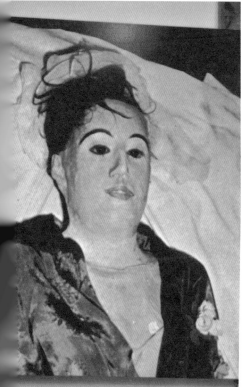

from Hemingway House, so why not? You can climb to the top of the 86 foot tower for a good view and photo opportunity. The lighthouse was built in 1847; the light extinguished in 1969, then restored in 1989, giving the light another life.

The **East Martello Museum** is on South Roosevelt Boulevard, near the entrance to the airport. This Civil War fort was built in 1862 as a defense against the Confederate Army but never saw military action. Highlights include Robert, the haunted doll, a sponger's diving outfit, photos of the corpse Elena, and the bizarre, welded, scrap metal art of Stanley Papio, found in the museum's citadel (pictured on previous page). Don't miss that. The museum is dank, dusty, tacky, odd, and a bit spooky actually. Some claim it's haunted. Kid's will like this place but may find it perplexing; guide them up the twisting, narrow stairs of the citadel. An adult ticket is $6; kids over 6 go for $3.

**The Custom House** now houses the **Key West Museum of Art and History** at 281 Front Street. It's the huge red brick building near Mallory Square, now aesthetically assaulted and surrounded by the adjacent Westin, built not many years ago. The Custom House, built in 1891, was the government center, post office, and court house during Key West's golden years as one of the wealthiest towns in the nation. You'll see the art of Mario Sanchez and Paul Collins, learn more about pirates, the *USS Maine*, Hemingway, and follow the history of the island through the best and worst of times. This is a more formal and straightforward museum than the quirky one at East Martello. History buffs should visit both for perspective. Adults go for $10, kids over 6 for $5.

The tour of the **Harry S. Truman Little White House** is quite out of step with what one comes to expect of Key West, but there it is, a presidential museum in the midst of all this partying, paradise, and conch and rooster stuff. Harry spent 175 days of his presidency (1945-1952) here, swimming, fishing, playing poker, and playing the host. The presidential digs remain as they were furnished in 1949, and anyone who grew up in the Forties and Fifties are likely to experience recovered memories—the forgotten lampshades, carpet, chairs and table settings of childhood homes. The guides here are particularly well versed and entertaining, showing who sat where at important dinners, explaining sleeping arrangements, pointing out the famous "The buck stops here" plaque. Besides Truman, Eisenhower spent time here, as did Kennedy and the Clintons. Members of "the greatest generation" love this tour. It's perfect for a rainy day, but get here before the cruise ship crowds.

"The World Famous" **Conch Tour Train**, and of course there are several of them, crawl around the island like centipedes, bewildered and hopeful new arrivals looking out from under the festive awnings above the cars. This is the sort of thing so many of us avoid, so conspicuously touristy; we don't want to be among the pasty snowbirds in shorts and black socks clutching plastic bags filled with t-shirts. Nevertheless, go. The train is an odd thread in the fabric of the island, a queer note in the daily music, a metaphor for the cheesy, filled with good intent. Your train engineer's jokes will seem canned, the facts skewed, yet this is a good initial orientation—a prelude to your biking and walking adventures. Even years later, when you've been here many times, when you spend winters here, maybe own a place, it's good to step onto the train again. You will be reminded how wonderfully baffling this place can be.

The **Key West Aquarium** at 1 Whitehead Street was part of the Federal Reconstruction of Key West in the 30s. This is not SeaWorld, but you can see eels, turtles, barracuda; you can watch the scheduled feedings and pet a living shark. The kids have a great time here. Drag queens, presidential digs, a writer's oeuvre rarely impress children. Fish, however pathetic, do—if they are moving.

Just a few blocks from busy Duval you'll find the **Florida Keys Eco-Discovery Center**. Here you'll find exhibits of the various reef environments, a mock-up of a hardwood hammock, interactive features, and the twice-hourly showing of *Reflections*, a beautiful film of the life on the reef. Admission is free and the center is open from 9:00 until 4:00 Tuesdays through Saturdays. You follow Southard as if you're going to Zachary Taylor Beach, four blocks southwest of Duval. In fact, stop here to or from your beach outing

The **Sunset Celebration** might generously be likened to the island's daily communal church service, the tipping point from the natural world with its sunlight, flying fish, and pastels to that more human, inner, darker world of the night, filled with the throb of music and wild laughter, framed by doors and windows lit with artificial light. Sunset marks the departure of the cruise ships and their transient guests and honors the committed who gather with their kids and lovers and cameras in a kind of pulling it all together at a party for the sun. Jugglers of knives, cats leaping through flaming hoops, a dog on a tightrope, performers in chains, on stilts, on fire, all ask for your attention and money, everyone biding their time until the top of that huge orange ball goes "plink!"—into the ocean as expected before everyone is released into the streets again with their disparate desires. It's crazy and fun and happens 365 days a year and locals rarely go, but do go at least once; kids love it and you will too. Follow the crowd to Mallory Square about an hour before sunset.

Pat Croce's **Pirate Soul** at 524 Front Street is the only Disney-esque thing on Key West. It's better than Ripley's Believe it or Not, and its theme has a direct connection with Key West's distant pass. Learn about Blackbeard, Captain Kidd, Calico Jack, life on the ships, weapons, devices of torture. The displays and interactive features are really excellent; this is a real museum and the material is quite extensive. You can sit in pitch darkness in the dungeon and hear a battle going on above you (children sometimes cry or bolt for the door). It's another great rainy day thing. Kids pay $8.55, adults $13.50.

**Art Galleries**—You could spend several days in Key West just on an art crawl. There are more than 50 galleries ranging from the expensive and ubiquitous Wyland and Thomas Kinkaid (Painter of Light!) stores, to the local and unique. Since George Bellows and John James Audubon, the Keys have been a great source of inspiration and interpretation for artists working in paint, sculpture, glass, photography, and ceramics. You'll also discover furniture from Java, stone sculptures from Zimbabwe, paintings from Haiti, and anything from "investment quality" pieces to souvenirs can be found, mostly along Duval or on White Street. Art lovers and collectors should pick up the Florida Keys Council of the Arts *Gallery Guide,* or the concise and well-illustrated *Key West Art Guide* for detailed

Art Studio

*Art is everywhere in Key West.*

maps and listings. The spectacular Sculpture Key West exhibit runs for several weeks starting in late January and features works (some huge) displayed at Fort Zach Taylor and throughout the city.

Anyone will enjoy a stop at the **Alan S. Maltz Gallery** at 1210 Duval. His photography of Florida Keys wildlife, people, water, sunsets and weather are remarkable. You can buy his award-winning coffee table books, and drool over the huge prints that make many consider throwing away their cameras. This is world class nature photography spectacularly displayed. Most people are viscerally moved by the work of Don Dahlke who does very evocative open windows, looking out into tropical vistas, and by the paintings of Thomas Arvid who does hard to believe  (his oils look like nearly impossible photographs) wine bottles and glasses. You can find these artists, along with Tripp Harrison and others at **A Boy and His Dog** at 619 Duval. The artwork of Bill Mack, "the finest relief sculptor in the world today," is honestly breathtaking and extraordinary.  You can see his sculpture at the very upscale **Luis Sottil Studios** at 716 Duval. The Noah's cigar oils (you can almost smell them), along with the edgy, very stylized party people of Todd White's imaginary world hang at **Black Pearl**, 826 Duval. More remarkable contemporary art can be seen at the **Charest-Weinberg, Kent**, and **Lucky Street** galleries, all on upper Duval. Sharon Wells, as much as any artist, captures in paint and photography the essence, the magic of Key West. Her **Key West Light Gallery** is at 1203 Duval.

**Nancy Forrester's Secret Garden** is off Simonton on Old School Lane across from Heron House.  This would have been a great place to play Tarzan as a kid, maybe now as well. The exotic plants and trees make it hard to believe you're still in Key West. It's another of those "falling through the looking glass experiences" one has here. Nancy has a small gallery in the midst of this hideaway.

**The Key West Butterfly & Nature Conservatory** at 1316 Duval is an educational experience, a gallery, and a conservatory which houses hundreds of butterflies from settings all over the world. You walk around in a little tropical jungle, the sound of tiny waterfalls all about, and the air filled with fluttering color. When you are finished you can buy decorative plastic cases of butterflies artistically arranged; just one butterfly, or if your budget allows, many butterflies fixed in an ascending wave. Butterflies live very short lives and this industry doesn't shorten them further, the staff will assure you.

The **Key West Tropical Forest** and **Botanical Garden** on Stock Island features the exotic plant life of South Florida, Cuba, and the Caribbean. Here you will see the Spanish Stopper, Strangler Fig, Blolly, Thatch Palm, Poisonwood Tree, the Dildo Cactus and the Paradise Tree. Many of the species are endangered. You will also see turtles and fish in the pool, lizards and butterflies along the mulched paths. This is a beautiful and quiet place to spend an hour or two. It's open daily. The suggested donation for adults is $5.00. Kids are free. From Key West you drive over to Stock Island and take a left at College Road. This is a good late morning stop before you head over to The Hogfish Bar and Grill for lunch.

Overheard conversation among tourists at the corner of Southard and Duval: "Well, which way is it to the water?"

"It's an island stupid, any direction!"

Midwesterners who rarely see the ocean should taste it, get a little on the tongue; life's blood, your Mother Earth. It is this taste of the sea that you feel in the oysters, the shrimp, when you cut yourself and bleed, when you have sex.

The **beaches** are cheap and easy, although not so great in Key West, but we'll start there. **Smathers** is the long and most populous beach along South Roosevelt. It looks like everyone's idea of a Florida beach—palm trees, hardbodies, volleyball, snack stands, flags blowing in the wind, sailboarders. But the water is often dirty, the swimming dubious. It's very busy during spring break and a good place for those people.

**Rest Beach** is the beach, just west, right after Smathers, along Atlantic Boulevard. It's something of a park too, more peaceful than Smathers. **Higgs Beach** is next and runs from the White Street Pier (and the AIDS Memorial) towards the curve inland at Reynolds Street. **South Beach** is the crowded but festive little beach at the end of Duval where you'll find the Southernmost Beach Club. **Dog Beach** is at the end of Vernon, adjacent to Louie's Backyard. It truly is for the dogs; good citizens keep an eye on their dogs and pick up after them.

The **Fort Zachary Taylor State Park and Beach** is an oasis of beauty and relative tranquility on the southwest corner of the island. You would never stumble upon it as you wander the city, but you might spy it from a day sail or snorkel trip, wondering what cool little beach that is, absent some looming hotel or congestion of volleyball players. To get there you drive, bike, or walk down Southard, through the Truman

annex. There is a little kiosk you pass in the middle of the street. Don't be shy or dissuaded. Pause, wave at the security guard, and proceed through the annex, then veer left to avoid the Navy pier, and go on to the park entrance. If you're on a bike or walking it will cost you $1.50, the best deal on the island.

Here is a strand of shimmering Atlantic water, picnic tables, the little Cayo Hueso Café—a snack bar really, featuring pizza, hot dogs, iced coffee, and a few adult beverages to be consumed on the deck only. You can rent lounges and umbrellas or equipment for the quiet sports—kayaks, snorkel gear. There are clean bathrooms and changing rooms and an outdoor freshwater shower. After you've cooled off in the water you can bike around, tour the Fort—fascinating for its Civil War era cannons and other artifacts. The beach angles down towards the water and consists of crushed coral and limestone—you'll need your Crocs to walk the beach and enter the water. (Cranky people on websites list the sharp-rocked beach and the rather long, hot walk to this place as annoyances; but it's a perfect destination for a bike ride.)

Everything in Key West, it seems, is the center of some controversy, and this little park is no exception. The commercial vendors here, the park service, certain planners are slowly removing the Australian Pines in favor of indigenous plants (the pines actually do whisper, and most of us really like them). Also there is talk of a pavilion out on the point, which, reason suggests, would block the view—and why a pavilion? It would facilitate certain functions it seems. Decency suggests leaving the place alone.

Perhaps the best way to see and feel the ocean is aboard one of the schooners that sail in the old style, quietly, leaning into the wind, a bit of spray coming over the bow. These are the ships, although replicas, which populate the dreams and history of Key West's past. The **Liberty, Liberty Clipper, Appledore, Hindu, Jolly II Rover**, and **Western Union** dock at the Historic Key West Bight. They operate on various schedules, but most offer afternoon and sunset sails with snacks and drinks. Far from the milling crowds, a few hours on the open sea on a schooner is one of the very best ways to spend an afternoon in Key West.

The best way to get into and to know the water is on one of the sail/kayak/snorkel tours. **Danger Charters**, my vote for best trip on the island, takes groups of 10-20 in their shallow bottomed skipjack sailboats, designed for getting close to the reef, the flats, the mangroves, for both snorkeling and kayaking. You actually get into the mangroves and explore a truly magical world in there. They supply all the equipment, instruction, lunch, and drinks. Danger also does a nightly wine tasting (eight wines!) sunset sail. Their kiosk and slip is at the pier at the Westin.

The **Sebago** catamarans dock at the Historic Seaport, the **Fury** ties up there and at the Ocean Key Resort and Westin marinas. They offer day sails with snorkeling and sunset sails with drinks and snacks. Both outfits offer all-day adventures as well, which include snorkeling, kayaking, and other activities—don't forget your sunscreen. These are really large vessels, they hold quite a crowd, and are sometimes referred to as "cattle boats." A half day trip runs about $45. When the boats are full, the sun high in the sky, the drinks flowing and everyone is milling about in wet bathing suits, it's a good place to make new friends.

**Blue Planet Kayak Eco-Tours** offers small group kayak tours that depart from shore on and near Key West—Boca Chica, for example. The tours are extremely informative; the guides will show and tell about the birds, tidal creatures, plants—even survival skills. Once you get some experience, Blue Planet will rent you a kayak ($40/day) for fishing or further exploration.

**Lazy Dog**—can provide guides and gear and is on Stock Island at Hurricane Hole Marina (Mile marker 4). They can set you up with kayak tours, and everything you need when you want to go it alone, whether around Key West or out to The Tortugas. They also book flats and deep sea fishing trips and have a great store.

There are several small sailboat operators who cater to a more private and upscale experience. The folks at the sloop **Blue Ice**, located at the Key West Bight Marina will take you and up to five others on half or full day sails. Snorkeling, dolphin watching, leaning into the wind out on the Gulf Stream can be yours for $700 for the full day trip. Snacks and drinks provided. **Dream Catcher** is operated by Coastal Sailing Adventures. The 70 foot schooner is available for private multi day or shorter trips. A half day trip for 10 runs about $1000. This outfit also offers sail training for groups of adults and young people.

There are numerous **Scuba Diving** operators in Key West. **Lost Reef Adventures, Reef Raiders, Key West Diving Society**, and **Dive Key West** offer discount packages, instruction, and full and half day trips to various reef and wreck sites.

You can fish on the flats for jack, tarpon, permit, bonefish; or out in the Gulf for the monster pelagics (tuna, sailfish, marlin). Charters can be found at the

Garrison Bight or Key West Bight. Jumping rays, tarpon, sharks, bird life, and the infinite colors of the water make the trips about more than fish. Although you can have fun on one of the large group boats which are not too expensive, serious fishing costs serious money, $400-$1000 for a half to full day trip for up to four people. Catching (and releasing) a 250-pound marlin can be the thrill of a lifetime. In "The Ahab Complex," writer Philip Caputo says, "The blue marlin is to the Gulf Stream what the lion is to the Serengeti: it is the living symbol of its world, the beauty, might, and mystery of the Stream made flesh."

If the weather is hot and the wind is not strong, and you have the time and funds, a trip to the Dry Tortugas might be the highlight of your vacation. Take the historical tour, snorkel, walk the grounds. You can even camp overnight if that appeals to you. This is also

a phenomenal birding area. Bring binoculars. These last keys lie some 70 miles southwest of Key West. The main island is mostly occupied by Fort Jefferson, the imposing brick Civil War structure, leaving some beach area, and shady palmy oasis. The quickest way to The Tortugas is by **Seaplanes of Key West**, which depart from the airport, offering two round-trip flights a day, less than an hour's flight over the reef and sharks and wrecks below. Or you can take a ferry, **Sunny Days** and **Yankee Freedom**. A round trip will cost about $120 and includes lunch and snorkel gear. The seaplane trip is quicker, costs more, and robs you of a great day at sea if you like that sort of thing, and would like some time to nap or work on your tan. Once, on one of the ferries, I saw flying fish erupting from the waves, their little fins buzzing like wings. They'd disappear into the water, then appear again alongside the boat, a high speed squadron of fish out of water. Truly remarkable. Like so many things I've seen in Key West, they were something I'd never seen before, and haven't seen since.

*After snorkeling, cocktails aboard Sebago.*

# 8

# *Love, Sex & Romance*

Travel carries with it the desire for romance, an encounter with the new and different, the thrill of fresh experience. And, although romantic longings are not limited to love and sex, they are uppermost in the hearts and minds of men and women, young and old, who encounter a place as bizarre and promising as Key West. This island bristles with sensuality— warm nights, pulsing music, stars, moon, sun, rum, the rhythmic turning of the ceiling fan over your bed of flowers. Everything, it seems, is permitted. And possible. Depending upon your situation, the focus of your observations, and your value system, you may find Key West tremendously romantic, sensual, kinky, or disgusting.

This chapter will address three areas of concern. First, is Key West a good choice for a romantic vacation with my sweetheart? Yes, it is—with a few cautionary alerts. Next, is this a good place for singles? What are the odds? Yes to that as well; and we'll address odds. And finally, isn't Key West a very Gay place—what's with *that*?

Couples come to Key West to celebrate or rejuvenate their union—newlyweds, the "ran-off-withs," the trysts, anniversaries, lovers from Grand Forks who have fled the security of their electric blankets in the 30 below nights. If you are like-minded, travel well together, are in a happy and stable relationship, Key West is a wonderful getaway for such people. Cocktails and sun by the pool, affirming sunsets, mornings in bed, recreation at your leisure, salt on each other's skin—you go with the flow on island time. If, however, there are cracks in your relationship, you are off-sync somehow, Key West, rather cracked and off-sync itself, might make things worse. Fraught with temptation, this place challenges middle class ethics and family values, cub scouts and the two car garage.

If one or both of you have a problem with alcohol, it will grow wild here—a party through any open door, free drinks on every cruise in the harbor. And if you have other issues—wandering eyes, say, or more credit cards than are good for you—the various distractions of skin and leather, the lack of moral guidance may be a prelude to disaster. Stunning examples of domestic unraveling at 3:00 a.m. are a common feature of the police report in *The Citizen*.

Here are some Key West favorites to make the hearts grow fonder. Stay in one of the nicer, more spacious inns; one with privacy and gardens, a pool, time and space to be mostly alone. The Gardens Hotel, The Mermaid and the Alligator, and Heron House would be among your best choices.

If you prefer a "real" hotel, Pier House has a nice private, though small, beach, spa services, and great views of the water.

Take the sunset cruise on the Schooner Liberty. The snapping sails, the roll of the ocean, the salty breeze and the sinking sun will resonate with your biological impulses, your animal desires. On another night have a sunset cocktail at The Top of the La Concha hotel. Look down upon the bustle of Duval, the twinkling lights amidst the greenery.

Louie's, classy and intimate, on the water, with the lapping waves, would be a top choice for romantic dining. La Trattoria at 524 Duval is sometimes voted "best romantic" by the various guides. One of their ads mentions the "low lights, crisp white linens, and an intuitive staff who knows just when to pour the wine and when to let you savor it. That's Amore!" After your meal you can go to Virgilios's, the patio bar in the back, for jazz, blues and one of their specialty cocktails, the "Sexy Cherry Bomb," or the "Foreplay."

Adventuresome couples should consider **Senses at Play** (sensesatplay.com; 305-294-5008). John and Bernadette McCall, "premier erotic artists," operate a studio for couples of all kinds to be photographed in intimate settings. At Senses at Play you can arrange for a shoot of you and your lover in settings indoors and about the island. The McCalls do not photograph actual sex; they want to be clear about that. And a photo shoot isn't cheap. A three hour session will run $650. They provide drinks, candles, various settings, and conversation to get you relaxed, and a 55-image DVD with music background. The deluxe four hour session includes a fantasy girl if you like, and two 55 image DVDs. The very satisfied clients include couples both straight and gay.

Perhaps the most ubiquitous question in the mind of the potential new visitor is this: "I am single (or pretending to be). What are my chances in Key West?" If you are single, looking for love, and young, spring break is when you should come, but it is the one time I would never come—adolescent shrieking, angst, buddy binging, broken bottles thrown down the streets in the wee hours of the morning, naked youngsters in the pool, a patina of half digested pizza floating on the surface. The chance of getting lucky during the weeks of spring break, which seems to get longer with each passing year, is very high. The chance of remembering such luck is nil.

Mature adults might meet someone with like interests at a literary event or the boat races or just on holiday, but most travelers come here quite coupled. Key West has 55 men for every 45 women. The mean age is 39. This would paint a rosy picture for single straight women except for the fact that so many of the men are gay. For straight men, the prospects would seem dim indeed, a poor ratio, and many of the women gay as well. The gays have an advantage.

At any given time there are lots of singles here; local working people of all ages, tourists from all over the globe, divorced women traveling with Mom, guys fishing. The *"Bar Tab"* lists The Lazy Gecko as a good singles bar; Irish Kevin's, just next door, is wildly festive and just as good. Sloppy Joe's too is packed and vibrating with the dancing, but here everyone seems to be coupled. The sunset cruises and the crowded snorkeling boats are a good bet, the swimming and drinking lubricating the interaction. Then there is **Fausto's Food Palace** where you are aided in your selection by what a person might have in their cart. If I were single, looking for love, I'd come to Fausto's for each day's groceries, linger, and collect data on the regulars while I checked the fresh produce or the wine selection.

You might check out the crowd around the pool at **The Southernmost House**. For a $5 pass you can use the bar and pool at one of the most picturesque spots on the island. Neighbors sometimes complain about this pool pass business, saying the crowds get a bit rowdy and noisy in the late afternoons, something in your favor. For late night outings, **Upstairs at Mangoes** at 700 Duval advertises itself as Key West's premier dance club (on Saturday nights at 11:00). **Dante's Restaurant and Raw Bar** at 951 Caroline celebrates Service Industry Day on the last Tuesday of each month. Luck is where you find it, of course, and you might find it anywhere in Key West.

If you are single (or not) and not looking for love, but looking, there are three or four strip clubs in town, the most famous, **Teasers** on Duval. Being the paradise it is, the dancers come to Key West from all over the world—Argentina, Venezuela, Russia, Indianapolis. High roller types spend a great deal of money here. Many of the women are stunning, and the ones who know how to work the crowd might approach a six-figure outcome in lap-dance sales. Be aware though that *The Citizen* occasionally reports that a Mr. Smith from Cleveland reported the loss of his wallet, cash, and credit cards, after accompanying home someone claiming to be an exotic dancer, enjoying the pleasures of tropical passion, then waking to ruin. It's hot here, nobody wears much, and you need to go home, so be careful. The ATM may be your enemy.

The **Garden of Eden** is the clothing optional bar on the rooftop of the Bull and Whistle Bar just up the block from Sloppy's. The second floor of the Bull and Whistle is still the Bull and Whistle, the balcony bar. Keep your clothes on. From there you climb up the last set of stairs, encounter yet another bouncer at the top, and there you are—a high hedge, tables, and drinks under the stars. You are not *required* to take your clothes off. You can look around, but it's not nice to stare. About half the people are in some state of undress, a few naked, but the kind of people you'd like to see naked are never here.

You'll find the people you'd like to see naked at **Living Dolls** on Fleming. This place advertises personal one-on-one lap dances in private rooms. Fees and tips run around $350 an hour. The sign says that you, as well as the "dancer," are allowed to be naked. One wonders if this is legal. Or hygienic.

Key West is internationally known as a Gay Mecca, a place where "closets have no doors." Tennessee Williams may have sown the seeds, but the gay and cultural revolution of the 60s established Key West as the place to come for gays, lesbians, queens, and transgenders. It's the weather, of course, and Key West's wide open attitude about everything. Much is permitted and possible, over the top really—raucus gay bars, cabaret shows, pool parties, skinny dipping cruises, tea dances, clothing optional guesthouses, gay bingo, drag queen parades. Not everything about gay Key West is tropically hot and naughty. More conservative gay couples, visitors and residents, feel most welcome. And the permanent gay population of Key West is a major cultural force in the town's restoration, preservation, service and health industries, local charities and humanitarian efforts. Much of the island's class, style, art, theater, music, and tasteful tidiness is due to the gay members of the One Human Family.

Phobics and very conservative people sometimes express hesitation about visiting Key West, fearing having to witness that of which they do not approve, nervous about the possibility of being hit on by a same sex person. They should know that Key West is wild and strange in ways beyond gay; their disapproval will keep them very busy. My advice to them: If you suspect a gay person is talking to you, make eye contact, speak in a normal tone of voice, and back away slowly. Gays rarely attack unless provoked.

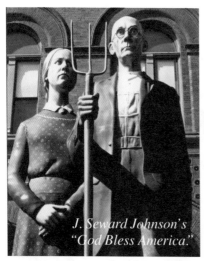

J. Seward Johnson's "God Bless America."

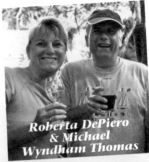

Roberta DePiero
& Michael
Wyndham Thomas

J. Seward Johnson
& Carolyn Mackler

Rosalind
Brackenbury

George Cooper
& Judy Blume

Charles Trumbull

Billy Collins

Will Weaver

Allen Meece

Curt Richter
& Perry Arnold

Rachael Estrada-Ryan
& Junot Diaz

Sheri Lohr

Barry George

*Artists and writers, visitors and residents.*

# 9
# Writers in Key West
## The Best Words in the Right Place

On a day of bicycling in January I nearly ran into Judy Blume, also on a bicycle, near the cemetery. Later on the same day I saw Robert Stone coming out of a bookstore on Simonton. And before the afternoon was over I'd also seen Billy Collins and Joyce Carol Oates walking down different streets. Four icons of American literature; yet this was not unusual for Key West.

Key West is a writer's soul's home, a circus of the imagination; attracting them to this place without actively doing so (no special tax breaks, inducements, recruiting parties). Long before the Literary Seminar, the Frost and Hemingway Festivals, the Studios of Key West and the various workshops currently running, writers have come here, more often quietly than not, for a short time or a lifetime.

The roll call includes Poets Laureate, National Book Award Winners, Pulitzer and Nobel winners—novelists, journalists, tellers of stories in fact or fiction, cartoonists, composers, playwrights, illustrators, editors, publishers. There is hardly any other worthy human activity where so many like minds are drawn to such a tiny place to either be with others or alone. One can approximate the reasons this is so, but the real reason, not reasonable at all, is that there is, truly, some kind of magic here, angels, dark and white.

The writers who have lived or have spent considerable time here represent a large and very recognizable piece of the canon of modern American literature: John Dos Passos, Elizabeth Bishop, Wallace Stevens, Tennessee Williams, Robert Frost, John Hersey, Richard Wilber, Annie Dillard, Philip Caputo, Allison Lurie, . . . and as these writers come immediately to mind, so do scores of others that we've studied, read in class, in a book, or in *The New Yorker*.

Many others, residents or frequent visitors, are impressive for the wide variety of their offerings: Gore Vidal, Jerry Herman (*Hello Dolly!* and *La Cage Aux Folles*), Truman Capote, Shel Silverstein, Gahan Wilson, Hunter S. Thompson, James Leo Herlihy (*Midnight Cowboy*), Harold Robbins, Stephen King, Jim Harrison (*Legends of the Fall*), and scores of others – all on this island of fewer than 30,000 residents on seven square miles.

Without Ernest Hemingway's presence and influence, Key West would not be what it is today. Much of his best writing was done here, but it was his other activities that defined an era for many men and women in the early decades of the last century; the African safaris, battling the huge marlin out on the Gulf Stream aboard the *Pilar*, the adventures of war and bullfighting, his association with Gary Cooper, Jack Dempsey, and other luminaries of his time (Marlene Dietrich, Picasso). It has been fashionable in circles both literary and cultural to dismiss Ernest Hemingway as a cliché of "the man's man." It is that judgment that is the cliché. Although he behaved badly at times (though certainly no worse than the superstar sports and music idols of today), he wrote some of the clearest, truest, most heartbreaking prose in the English language.

*A Hemingway Marlin in Sloppy Joe's,*

*Key West Writing Room*

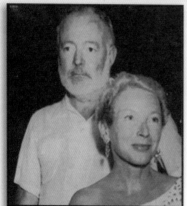

*Earnest and Mary Hemingway –*
*his 4th and last wife, in Cuba*

*On the deck of the Pilar,*
*Earnest's fighting chair.*

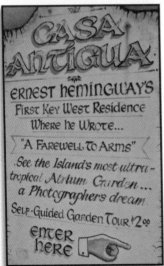

CASA ANTIGUA
ERNEST HEMINGWAY'S
First Key West Residence
Where he Wrote...
"A Farewell To Arms"
See the Island's most ultra-
tropical Atrium Garden...
a Photographers dream
Self-Guided Garden Tour $2.00
ENTER HERE

*House on Whitehead Street*

Read if you have not, *A Moveable Feast*, then *The Old Man and the Sea*. Some of his least read, but best prose, can be found in the factual account of bullfighting in *Death in the Afternoon*.

Much of the wave of popularity that washed over Key West in the years following World War II—until, perhaps the 80s—was due to Ernest Hemingway, his writing, and a style of life that was no longer possible or accepted. The tradition of the sportsman/writer has been carried on more recently by such excellent novelists and journalists as Thomas McGuane (married to Jimmy Buffet's sister), Philip Caputo, and Jim Harrison—all Key West aficionados.

The **Key West Literary Seminar**, created by David Kaufelt, has been the anchor literary event on the island for twenty five years. Held in January, it brings together writers and readers, focusing on a different topic each year—Hemingway; The American Novel; The Memoir; Writers and the Natural World; Humor; The Literature of Adventure, Travel, and Discovery; New Voices. The topic of the 2009 seminar is Historical Fiction, bringing writers like E.L. Doctorow, Alan Gurganus, Gore Vidal, and Andrea Barrett.

One day you are on a plane headed for Key West, reading a bestseller. A few hours later you're in line at the buffet at the Lighthouse Museum, chatting with the author of your reading, perhaps Pico Iyer, Calvin Trillin, Garry Trudeau, Frank McCort, or Peter Mattheissen. If you have bookish friends back home, you can make them jealous by name-dropping upon your return to the landscape of ice and snow. I do.

I was sitting in the audience at Tennessee Williams Fine Arts Center, listening to James Merrill talk about Key West as an inspiration for writers and artists. He spoke about the heat, the fecundity, the end of the road thing. His comments were wonderful, but even more wonderful were the notes the man next to me was taking down. The phrases and comments were as good as what we were hearing from Merrill. I began to take notes on this man's notes, trying to be inconspicuous. When Merrill was finished he introduced the next poet —former Poet Laureate and two-time Pulitzer winner Richard Wilbur. The man sitting next to me said, "Please excuse me," then got up and proceeded to the stage.

At an opening-night cocktail party on the grounds of the East Martello Museum, I was invited into a circle of men standing by the bar, James Boatwright, then editor of *Shenandoah*, among them. The conversation was extremely literate and wide ranging, and I tried to keep up, Jack Daniels in hand. Then, it seemed, everyone was going to a party. Come along, they said. Feeling quite out of my league, in only my first hours ever on the island, and in a group like this, and a bit done in by the generous portions of Jack, I declined, said I needed to get back to friends. Okay, one of them said, but it will be fun—Susan Sontag is going to be there.

During a break at The Literary Seminar, in the cramped men's room on the first floor of the San Carlos Institute, I was in line with four or five men, waiting to use the urinal. I was annoyed really, wishing they would hurry, then realized I was the only one in there who didn't have either a Pulitzer, a National Book Award, or the honor of being a past Poet Laureate of the United States.

I am gushing shamelessly, but as an avid reader since childhood, and a college English major, many of the best hours of my life have been spent in the gardens and on the porches of Key West, chatting with people like Peter Taylor, Gretel Ehrlich, Rick Bass and Russell Banks, and especially the other enthusiastic fans of books and writing who come from all over the world to this annual discussion and celebration.

Miles Frieden has been the executive director of the seminar for many years and you'll find information at keywestliteraryseminar.org.

The **Robert Frost Poetry Festival** is a more low key event and has been held in April for the past 14 years in the gardens of the Heritage House Museum— home of the Robert Frost Cottage. Repeat guests and writing workshop facilitators have included Key West poet and fiction writer Rosalind Brackenbury, Lee Gurga and Charles Trumbull—editors of *Modern Haiku*, Barry George, and Michael Wyndam Thomas, Poet-at-Large of the Conch Republic, Frost scholar, and playwright from Worchester England. The five day affair consist of writing sessions (appropriate for beginning poets and writers, as well as those already published), readings, cigar smoking and wine tasting, and a sunset sail with readings and music and the pouring of adult beverages. Literature on the high seas. Reef Perkins, Vice Admiral of the Conch Republic, husband of Festival Director Roberta Di Piero, leads everyone in baudy pirate verse.

**Hemingway Day**s, held in mid to late July, goes from the informal to the zany. Maybe it's the heat and humidity. There is the famous look-alike contest, a corny "running of the bulls" event, arm wrestling, legitimate readings and theatrical presentations. There is a short story contest and a 5K run, and men everywhere are smoking cigars; some of the women too.

**The Studios of Key West**, at 600 White Street,

offers exhibits, workshops, and lectures in writing and the visual arts. Its mission is to provide a sense of support and community to local and visiting writers, painters, sculptors, photographers, publishers, critics, and historians; a place to share work and perspective. The museum, offering a variety of exhibits, is open to the public.

*Captain Tony Terracino with the secret of salt publisher Kim Narenkivicius, left, and editor and writer Cricket Desmarais.*

***The secret of salt: an indigenous journal***, published by artist and photographer Kim Narenkivicius, is a biennial journal of Key West writers and artists, the residents and transients, their visions and words, expressing the varieties of Key West imagined and experienced: Eric Anfinson, Letty Nowak, Marie Cosindas, Kirby Congdon, George Murphy, Francis Masat, Jeffrey Cardenas, Cricket Desmarais, Barbara Bowers, Margit Bisztray. In a review in *Key West Magazine* (March, 2007), Sam Schneider sees the intent of the journal as "to document the writings and images that constitute today's 'Key West School' before the island sheds its image one more time."

A literary landmark is **Key West Island Bookstore** at 513 Fleming. They carry new, used, and rare books, many signed by the authors who have made the island famous. This is a browser's bookstore, a rainy day bookstore; disheveled, cramped, the scent of all the printed pages enough to keep you here or bring you back again and again. So many books, so little time.

**Voltaire Books** at 330 Simonton is smaller, newer, and very tidy. They host frequent readings and book-signing events. A live radio newsmagazine is broadcast from here every Sunday featuring local artists, officials and (of course) eccentrics.

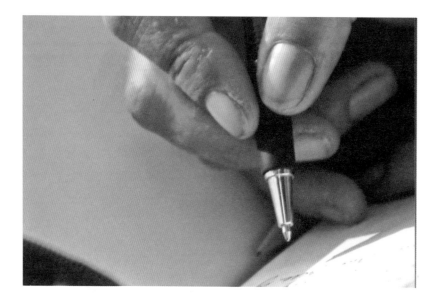

Writing, in the end, is a solitary venture, done at the cottage in the woods, in an apartment somewhere, behind a closed door, in the little room the writer carries around in his or her head. But for gathering in the name of writing, Key West is the best place of all.

# 10
## *Leaving Key West*

There are many Key Wests. Each time I have come here, I find a slightly different one, some disagreeable (windy with highs only in the sixties, this flight of tourists unbearable, everything as crass and commercial as anywhere else, the characters and crackpots too posturing), but others just as alluring and surprising as the one I fell in love with the first time. I decided not to return after some early visits. But something pulled me back—the memory of a leopard ray rising out of the water, the sunset's tricks, the gaudy allure of the music-filled nights, the suggestive allusions on menus, gravestones, want ads, whispered secrets at any bar in town.

Key West is a microcosm of both our personal journeys and our national history: the aspirations and loss of dreams, our failures of plumbing, transit, and structural integrity; our vulnerability to time and weather, the shortage of money, our quest for love and fame, riches and beauty, our longings for immortality.

Key West is both much larger and smaller than you first imagine—so small town in some ways—yet very connected with the larger world of art, travel, commerce, and politics. It is a community of great charity and cooperation, yet everyone is scrapping for survival, a foothold: the homeless on the beach, the poet in the turret, the innkeeper, the sushi chef, everyone trying to write themselves a good story, find a lover, sail a ship.

This is a very difficult place to come without "making it" somewhere else first if "making it" is your goal. If you come and expect to live on hourly wages you will, like many, need to have three or four jobs and share a small apartment with other people. New restaurants, galleries, kitty boutiques, come and go with great regularity. To buy a house or start a business here you need a six figure balance in your checkbook, then a great deal of luck, energy, and talent. Only a few writers and artists emerge from here, *sui generis*; most come from somewhere else.

Others come here with little and manage to hang on, integrate themselves into the local fabric without the need to succeed in the traditional sense; live a smaller life in a large way—one of the lessons one might learn here. The life of the Cassiopeia jellyfish, not that of the shark or barracuda.

When you have visited here enough times you come to understand why many who leave here come back. Key West is like the bad boy or girl that gets under your skin; difficult, unreliable, fascinating, disappointing, sexy, needy and surprising in so many more ways than one individual could ever be; and so this becomes the only place to be, to feel most truly alive, most truly home.

You may be among the many who don't really care for Key West. There are more than enough reasons. Its streets are directionless, nothing is black and white, there is little concern for right and left, and if you stay here, or come back often, you come to understand that the journey doesn't start until after you arrive—the very reason drawing many of us back.

I have come to realize that this guidebook is a journey, never finished, never wholly true, and for that I ask your understanding. I would like to apologize and beg for forgiveness in the omission of restaurants, coffee shops, inns, gardens, galleries, charters and guides, and people who are as deserving of space and mention as any other listed in these pages. I thank all the bartenders, waiters, boat crews, shopkeepers, innkeepers, and fellow travelers for their suggestions and information, for giving excellent conversation.

In particular, credit goes to Arrow Printing and Barb Van Thomma for the cover design, layout, and printing of this book, to Tammi Hartung for her meticulous copy editing, to Cricket Desmarais in Key West for guidance in matters of style and fact, the "luminous particulars" of Key West, and to all the writers and friends, mothers, lovers and dogs whom I've brought to Key West, hope to bring to Key West, or whom I've left behind when called.

# 11
# A Glossary of Miscellany

*Odds and ends, trivia, bonus features, washed up on shore, the pickings of roosters, found in the bougainvillea . . .*

**Aquarium** – It's not large or wondrous, but it's very reef-relevant and quite educational. On a recent visit I learned that the Jewfish has been renamed the Goliath Grouper as of 2001.

**Bight** – A bend or curve, a small bay between two points of land. The Key West Bight, the "Historic Seaport," is the harbor or marina area where you find Conch Republic Seafood Company, The Schooner Wharf Bar, many of the tall masted schooners, fishing charters, snorkel boats. The Tortugas Ferries come and go from here. There is another bight, the Garrison Bight on Palm Avenue where you'll find many fishing charters. Harbors, marinas, bights—the terms confuse people from Iowa. Near the Truman Annex, on the west end, there is the Cruise Ship Mole. Mole? It looks like a harbor or bight to me.

**Boca Chica** – The Key before Stock Island, site of the Naval Air Station. It's so odd, just ten miles from your destination in paradise you see giant cargo planes or fighter jets circling just above you, practicing touch and goes at the big out-of-sight runway.

**Bougainvillea** – The common, very proliferative flowering plant exposing itself all over Key West in pink, magenta, red and orange. The viney, thorny thing can grow to over 30 feet and you see it climbing walls and fences, hanging out everywhere. Bikers and walkers who have had too much to drink often veer off the sidewalk into these plants, suffering tell-tale scratches.

**Captain Tony** – Tony Tarracino, bootlegger, gambler, charter boat captain, Cuban gun runner, former mayor of Key West, owner of Captain Tony's Saloon since 1958. His slogan: "All you need in this life is a tremendous sex drive and a great ego. Brains don't mean a shit." Last of the great genuine characters, Tony can still occasionally be seen on a stool in the bar that bears his name, signing the breasts of giddy tourist women.

**Cats** – They are always the subject of controversy, especially at the Hemingway House. The more benign debate is about the six-toed cats, whether or not they are the direct descendants of Ernest's cats. Lately, animal rights groups and various legal entities and people who have nothing better to do, wonder whether the cats at the house should come under rules governing zoos and other animal displays. The arguments are tedious.

**Chickens** – And the roosters who rule them could appear under things to do and see, what to eat, lodging (some guests complain of the clucking at night in certain locales and should be forewarned), the best of Key West (who else features them as an accessory?), and must be mentioned in any discussion of history (cockfighting) and politics. Many who live or visit here find them quaint, even essential. Some folks are indifferent unless one of the birds pecks at them or disturbs their breakfast at Blue Heaven. Many people (hypochondriacs, condo developers, insomniacs, pollophobics) view chickens as symbols of anarchy and want them eradicated.

**Churches** – Perhaps with all the conspicuous sinning, the general level of passion, the amount of wealth and sunshine focused in such a small area, it's not surprising that Key West would have so many churches—more than thirty. All faiths are represented.

**Cigars** – Most men, and some women, really want to smoke one when they are here; it's the Hemingway thing. And do get a photo of yourself with an appropriate background. You'll notice if you are just a very occasional cigar smoker that the cigars here, if freshly rolled, are actually moist, very aromatic and flavorful, and last a good hour or two, unlike ones in the cold and dry north which have the consistency of sawdust wrapped in paper. In any case, quit when you get dizzy.

**Coffee** – Five Brothers Deli and Grocery, at Southard and Grinnel, is the early morning spot to pick up your Cuban coffee. It's a local tradition and the perfect stop on your early morning bike ride. There are several coffee shops around town. Sippin' on Eaton—next to The Tropic Theater, features both computer based internet and wifi. They also occasionally host poetry readings. Plantation Coffee Shop over on Caroline is something of a literary hangout and an art gallery. Wifi and computer available as well. Great porches for conversation, writing, or waiting out a rain shower.

**Colors of Key West** – The film, *Key West – City of Colors* (available from Netflix) is an excellent documentary about the unfurling of the mile and a quarter long rainbow flag up Duval Street (from the Gulf, at 0 Duval, to the Atlantic and South Beach) on June 15th, 2003. More than 3000 volunteers walked Gilbert Baker's symbol of diversity (and

Gay Pride more particularly) from sea to sea. Key West was devastated by the AIDS epidemic of the 80s and 90s. The AIDS Memorial is adjacent to Higgs Beach at the White Street pier. The colors signify as follows: Purple – spirit, Blue – serenity, Turquoise – magic, Green – nature, Yellow – sunlight, Orange – healing, Red – life, Fuchsia – sex.

**Conch** – Conchs – the people (only those born in Key West). Conch —The Republic—established in 1982. Conch—the fritter, which are like crab cakes, with conch meat. Pronounced like "a conk on the head." See also, Queen Conch.

**Cruise Ships** – Key West became a Port O' Call (bauble and bathroom stop) for the cruise ship lines in a serious way in the late 1980s. As many as three of the floating cities bump up against the island on some days, hatching out as many as 4000 visitors into the streets of Key West. It keeps the Conch Train very busy. The ships block the sunset if they remain at the pier, and are fined if they do not leave by then. Still, sometimes, there they are, several stories high, the passengers looking down upon the very cranky celebrants and jugglers, dogs and fire-eaters, in the shadows below, while, on the other side of the ship, the sun sinks spectacularly into the ocean.

**Dogs** – Life is, in Key West, a dog's life, and the dogs here seem to enjoy their lives very much. The Schooner Wharf bar, for one, welcomes dogs, has water dishes for visiting dog, hosts dog birthday parties. Some of their shirts read "Hang with the Big Dogs." There is Dog Beach at the end of Vernon, near Louie's Backyard restaurant. Key West's leash law says you must have your dog under control; you don't really need a leash. You must clean up after your dog, however, and like anywhere, there are people who don't like dogs. Dogs always know who they are and it is these hard souls that they bark at, poop near, and generally behave badly around.

**Egret** – The long-legged birds you see all the way down the keys are not, it seems, just egrets. Some, although of the same family, are herons. The white phase of the great blue heron has yellow legs and is quite large, with a 72 inch wingspan. The great egret is a bit smaller, with black legs. The snowy egret is smaller still and has a black bill and bright yellow feet. The cattle egret is, again, smaller, 20 inches tall, with a yellow bill. There is also a reddish egret, a tricolor heron, the little blue heron, the green heron, others. Many inlanders give up bird watching, confused by the scores of various sparrows and finches; for coastal folks, the wading birds are just too much.

**Fantasy Fest** – This ten-day festival prior to Halloween (but more Mardi Gras than Halloween) is the busiest and highest revenue producing event of the year. Body painting, balls, costumes, pet parades, food and fetish events. Rooms are booked a year or more in advance. Of course.

**Faustos's** – It's the supermarket on Fleming. It's got a great deli, wine, sushi; a true Key West landmark. A great place to get supplies for the refrigerator in your inn, the cooler for the beach or fishing trip. In your flip-flops, shorts, and t-shirt, your bike chained up outside, you will feel like a local and, more than you might expect, this will give you a great rush of pleasure – much like when someone from a cruise ship asks you how to get to Hemingway's house.

**Films** – *Reap the Wild Wind* stars John Wayne as a Key West Wrecker. *Under the Twelve Mile Reef* stars Richard Boone and Robert Wagner as sponge divers; *To Have and To Have Not* is an adaptation of Hemingway's novel of the same name – set in Martinique instead of Key West to make it look more like *Casablanca*. *The Cuba Crossing* is about Captain Tony as a gun-runner. The beach at Fort Zachary Taylor plays the part of the Cuban Coast. The recent *Fools Gold* reveals mountains in the Florida Keys! And *Criss-Cross* stars Goldie Hawn working at Eden House, then turning stripper. The *Key West Picture Show* is a 40 minute film, silly and a bit dated, itself a parody of a travelogue, for sale around town —a fun souvenir.

***Florida Keys Paddling Guide*** – (By Bill Keogh) This is not a sex manual. It is both the best natural history guide on the keys, and a thorough paddlers' guide to this most remarkable and beautiful place—from Key Largo to Key West and on to the Dry Tortugas. Launching sites, charts, maps, and navigation information, extended trips, and descriptions of the flora and fauna above and below the water are all here. The book contains some anecdotes (flotsam and jetsam), personal philosophy, and would best be read as an enticement to your trip if you plan on some kayaking, months before you arrive here. I cannot recommend this book too highly.

**Frangipani** – Also called plumeria. The flowers of this shrubby tree are most fragrant at night, all the better to lure the sphinx moth for the purposes of pollination. But the flowers have no nectar, the odor a trick.

**Frigate Birds** – In North America these giant birds lay one egg in the spring only in the mangroves of the Dry Tortugas and the Marquesas. The bird is unmistakable, with a wingspan approaching six feet, the forked tail, and the sharply angled wings, resembling something designed by the defense department.

**Gentrification** – The up scaling of every structure, any piece of ground to something more profitable, characterized by exclusive boutiques—diamonds, watches, cologne, and million dollar condos.

**Ghosts** – Pirates, buried treasure, necrophilia, creaky old mansions, dark and very stormy nights, rum, madness and obsession; of course there are ghosts in Key West. The Original Ghost Tour departs nightly from the La Concha Hotel. The reviews are mixed and depend greatly on your luck with the guide.

**Gingerbread** – This is the decorative scroll-work found as trim on cornices, balustrades, on porches and balconies on old (and restored) houses. The decorative themes include bottles, pineapples, suits of cards, sometimes (historically) suggesting the activity to be found within. The style dates from the mid 1800s.

**Golf** – The Key West Golf Club, a 6500 yard Rees Jones designed course, is on Stock Island. Eighteen holes will cost you

$100 in the off season (summer), and about double that the other eight months of the year. You may be detained by the odd bird or reptile.

**Hangovers –** Don't have one when you plan on diving, snorkeling or sailing on windy days—especially diving. A good many diving accidents are linked to heavy festivities the night before. It's not easy to properly surface when you are vomiting at 40 feet underwater. On a lighter note, the local hangover guide suggests that a great way to deal with a hangover is frequent practice.

**Houseboat Row –** The drifters, the lost, the homeless, the most eccentric have always been with us, especially in Key West. Houseboat row, along South Roosevelt, once had dozens of grounded or barely navigable houseboats—complete with gardens, laundry lines, and rockers on the porch, floating upright, or not quite, among the mangroves. They were considered an eyesore by the genteel and only remnants of that lost tiny world remain. This subset of the population now wanders about the island, or out on Christmas Tree Island—just right (north) of ultra-upscale Sunset Key, a rather stunning juxtaposition of life's fortunes.

**Hammock –** A piece of land with hardwood trees on it. Such places are found on the keys, but those of us in the north often don't know the term so here it is. Key Deer live on Big Pine Key . . . in the hammocks.

**Hurricane –** The hurricane season is, officially, June 1st through November. Some hotels recommend you purchase traveler's insurance to protect your investment as there are no refunds for vacations interrupted by a Mandatory Evacuation Order. Insurance is not available for purchase once a storm is named. Thirty-six hurricanes have hit or passed by Key West since 1852, unearthing bodies at the first cemetery, spoiling Fantasy Fest, driving boats into the mangroves, blowing the vulnerable into bankruptcy. The airport is three feet above sea level. A perfectly aimed hurricane could blow everything into the ocean, leaving Key West as clean as a dinner plate.

**Jellyfish –** The Portuguese man-o'-war looks like a plastic bag, filled with air, bluish, with tentacles. The tentacles may be up to 70 feet long. They float on the surface of the water and are driven towards Key West from the Gulf Stream with strong south winds. They are the scourge of snorkelers, bathers and divers. The tentacles are venomous, the sting quite severe—like many bees if you tangle with the sticky tentacles. Charter operators and the beaches will announce warnings when these are around. Moon jellies, like foot-wide dished moons, float in groups, are quite pretty and delicate, and only mildly noxious. On your kayak adventure on the flats or near the mangroves you might see Cassiopeias or upside-down jellyfish lying upside down on the bottom. They are sunbathing and looking for food.

**Key Deer** – These mini-whitetails live mostly from No Name to Sugarloaf Keys. The males run about 80 pounds, a little bigger than half sized "normal" deer. They were listed as endangered in 1967, their numbers down to 50. Now, there are, perhaps, 800-900. In areas of their habitation the reduced highway speed limit is strictly enforced.

***Key West Reader*** – The *Key West Reader*, edited by George Murphy, is an anthology of some of Key West's most famous and representative writers: Elizabeth Bishop, Hemingway, Hunter Thompson, Richard Wilbur, Tennessee Williams. The collection, put together in 1989, is oddly eclectic (Hart Crane, Stephen Crane?), and has only twenty-five authors, but serves as an excellent introduction to literary Key West. I wish there had been additional volumes.

**Key Lime Pie** – Real key lime pie and the best key lime pie is simple—three egg yokes, sweetened condensed milk (one 14 ounce can), and one half cup of legitimate Key West lime juice (Nellie & Joe's or Kermit's). You beat this all together, pour it in a nine inch graham cracker crust pie shell and bake at 350 degrees for 15 minutes. Let it stand for ten minutes, then refrigerate until it's cold. You may sprinkle a bit of powdered sugar and cinnamon on top (like Vermouth in a real martini). Eat. Mmmmm. Don't foo foo it with whipped cream or chocolate or busier crusts. There is a lot of key lime pie in Key West, and like everything else it gets injected with too much theater, too much presentation, too many things on it which adorn the menu but not the pie.

**Library** – The Monroe Country Library on Fleming is clearly the library of a highly literate city. Tom Hambright in the history section knows or can find you anything about Key West. The Friends of the Library sponsor a rich series of lectures held at The Tropic Theater.

**Luggage, lost** – Because people are getting fatter and airlines must allow for this, and because the Key West runway is rather short (4801 feet), airlines will often take either you or your bags to Key West, but not both. Within a day or two the bags will arrive. Plan for this by bringing the essentials in your carry-on. That would be: money, credit cards, driver's license, shorts, flip-flops.

**Mahi-mahi** – It's also called dolphin, but not dolphin the mammal (novice sea fish eaters are often horrified noticing the item on the menu until they are enlightened). Very tasty and a good choice on the "catch of the day" menu, grilled or blackened.

**Mangroves** – "Complex trees in a simply magical place," says Bill Keogh in his paddling guide. It's what you see everywhere along the keys, on the land and from in the air. There are red, black, and white mangroves. Mangroves can desalinate seawater, function as a busy nursery for a tremendous variety of wildlife, and the seeds can survive nine months of drifting and may propagate continents away.

**Mile Markers** – Mile marker ZERO is at the corner of Whitehead and Fleming, at the courthouse, and is also marked with a sign reading "End of the Rainbow." The markers go up as you go east and then a bit north to Miami. You hit the mainland at about mile marker 110.

**Mopeds** – They are cheaply and aggressively rented here, and are a good way to get around, simple to park. They do make a lot of noise though and are a great source of income to orthopedic and plastic surgeons. If handled improperly or drunkenly they are a beacon to arresting officers. Don't do it. A bicycle could save you a few thousand dollars.

**Osprey** – You often see this most common raptor on your drive down the keys, as well as their nests, on the power poles or in the branches of dead trees. They dive into the water feet first for fish.

**Outré** – Eccentric, bizarre; the best word to describe Key West. A good cocktail party word.

**Poinciana** – The Royal Poinciana, also know as The Flamboyant Tree, must certainly feel at home in Key West. It features a large four-petaled flower in vivid red or orange yellow. An excellent shade tree, it grows 15 to 30 feet in height.

**Pool, city** – A great pool, perhaps Olympic sized, but rarely used. At the corner of Catherine and Thomas. No bar service; maybe that's why.

**Queen** – As in Dairy, there is one on United Street. Dairy Queen, Inc. had its convention here in 2007. They did not elect a Dairy Queen, despite the golden opportunity. As in drag, you'll find them on upper Duval near the 801 Bourbon Bar. The Queen Conch, the shell of the Republic, is pink on the inside and an endangered species.

**Reef** – Here is the only living coral reef in the United States. It is fragile and impacted by global warming, clumsy snorkelers, errant ships and other watercraft, polluted runoff from the Everglades, and farming. Kayaking, snorkeling and diving are the best ways to get to know the reef.

**Sharks** – Nurse sharks and lemon sharks are common in the Keys and the largest of them may be ten feet long. Hammerheads are sometimes seen. Sharks rarely bother anybody down here.

**Shopping** – Be aware that the area around Mallory Square, thick with cruise ship disgorgees, is fraught with quick and profitable commerce: gold, ice cream, T shirts, seashells, cigars. Watch out for credit card scams. Places unique to Key west include Leathermaster on Applerouth Lane (harnesses, erotic toys, lotions), a Kite Shop, dog and cat boutiques, Besame Mucho which claims: "Shop here and your life will be a joy forever." Go ahead, see if that's true.

**Stock Island** – is the next island up from Key West; Key West's mud room, utility center, and dump. Long ago a true stockyard, it's now home to the Botanical Gardens, the hospital, the golf course, less fancy marinas, Hogfish Bar and Grill, some secretive artists' studios, and the Tennessee Williams Fine Arts Center. There are some post-apocalyptic junkyards and trailer parks harboring vicious guard dogs, and methheads who resemble people in *The Dead* film series and who will get you if you are in the wrong place after dark.

**Theater** – The Red Barn Theater at 319 Duval has featured an eclectic series of plays and reviews, from December into April, since 1979. Some of the shows are written by Key Westers such as Shel Silverstein. The Waterfront Playhouse, now going strong for almost 70 years, is located near Mallory Square and offers drama, musicals, comedy. The Tennessee Williams Theater at the Florida Community College on Stock Island offers plays, musical performers, Broadway productions, and the performances of the Symphony, the Pops, the Chorale.

**Tipping** – Your bartender, waitperson, the person who attends to your room, the boat crew—all serve you cheerfully at their own economic peril. Many of these people have another job, maybe a third. You think this is an expensive place to visit? Try living here. Tip generously.

**Tropic Cinema** – One of the best things to happen in recent years is the formation of The Key West Film Society and the renovation of Tropic Cinema on Eaton, just off Duval. Dedicated to show the best in documentary, foreign, independent and other quality films, this is a gem of a

theater for the film buff. The Tropic and the KWFS also host special events, receptions, fundraisers, and kids' programs. Great popcorn, a wine bar, very comfortable seating. Movies in paradise.

**Turtles** – Five of the eight species of sea turtle can be found in the keys. You'll mostly likely see a loggerhead turtle, if any, while fishing or snorkeling, or sailing. They are all protected now. The Turtle Kraals is at the site of the old turtle slaughter docks. The green turtle, now uncommon, was the tastiest.

**Universe, Mr.** – Joe Universe conducts the stars and moonlight trip aboard the schooner *Liberty*. There is a slide show, coupled with use of a laser pointer to explain the history, positions, and lore about the constellations. The tiny lights far away on the horizon—that's Key West. Mr. Universe is a real astronomer but does not reveal another name. Many of the people here are from somewhere else, where they had a different name.

**Wind Chill** – Concerning all the colder-back-home stories: Shut your mouth. All the bartenders, all the boat crews, EVERYBODY hears these stories ALL DAY LONG, ALL WINTER LONG; THEY'VE HEARD THEM! Half of the people crawling around here in January and February are ALSO from Williston, North Dakota; Barron, Wisconsin; Buffalo, New York; and snow–up–your–ass Vermont. Key Westers know these stories all the way down to 60 below zero (Tower, Minnesota). That's why they are here and not where you live. They don't need to be reminded.

***Walking & Biking Guide*** – An extremely detailed and thoroughly researched guide to your Old Town exploration. More than a dozen walking and biking tours, by area, street, subject matter, are offered here. Author Sharon Wells owns the KW Light Gallery at 1203 Duval. The guide is free in Key West or may be ordered at www.seekeywest.com.

**Wisteria** – The purple, pink, white, or violet flowers are pendulous (sort of like lilacs) and fragrant. Common in Key West.

**Zane Grey Creek** – Key West likes to claim Zane Grey as one of its visiting authors, but he spent most of his time up at the Long Key fishing camp, near where a creek now bears his name. Grey was an occasional dentist, baseball player, philanderer, and writer of ninety (!) books, including *Riders of the Purple Sage*. Grey was an avid sportsman, early conservationist, and celebrity writer for *Outdoor Life* magazine.

# About the Author

Marsh Muirhead has been coming to Key West in all seasons, for all reasons, since 1986. He writes on a wide variety of topics for various magazines and newspapers. His fiction and poetry have appeared in *Carolina Quarterly, The Southeast Review, The Quarterly, Passager, Modern Haiku, the secret of salt,* and elsewhere. He lives on the banks of the Mississippi River in northern Minnesota.